THE OLD FARMER'S ALMANAC

VOLUME 7

YANKEE PUBLISHING INCORPORATED

***The Old Farmer's Almanac* Books**

Publisher: Sherin Pierce
Series editor: Janice Stillman
Art director: Colleen Quinnell
Managing editor: Jack Burnett
Contributors: Jack Burnett, Alice Cary, Tim Clark, Betty Earl, Mare-Anne Jarvela, Kathleen Kilgore, Barbara Mills Lassonde, George Lohmiller, Martie Majoros, Harry Edward Neal, Sandy Newton, Sarah Perreault, Louise Sandback, Stephanie Shaw, Janice Stillman, Heidi Stonehill

V.P., New Media and production: Paul Belliveau
Production directors: Susan Gross, David Ziarnowski
Production artists: Jennifer Freeman, Rachel Kipka, Janet Selle

Companion Web site: Almanac4kids.com

Digital editor: Catherine Boeckmann
New Media designers: Lou S. Eastman, Amy O'Brien
E-commerce manager: Alan Henning
Programming: Reinvented, Inc.

For additional information about this and other publications from *The Old Farmer's Almanac,* visit **Almanac.com** or call **800-ALMANAC** (800-256-2622)

Consumer marketing manager: Kate McPherson

Distributed in the book trade in the United States by Houghton Mifflin Harcourt and in Canada by Thomas Allen & Son Limited

Direct-to-retail and bulk sales are handled by Stacey Korpi, 800-895-9265, ext. 160

Yankee Publishing Inc., P.O. Box 520, 1121 Main Street, Dublin, New Hampshire 03444

ISBN: 978-1-57198-743-3

ISSN: 1948-061X

FIRST PRINTING OF VOLUME 7

Thank you to everyone who had a hand in producing this Almanac and getting it to market, including printers, distributors, and sales and delivery people.

PRINTED IN THE UNITED STATES OF AMERICA

HI, KIDS,

and Moms, Dads, Aunts, Uncles, Grandparents, and Teachers everywhere!

Welcome to ***The Old Farmer's Almanac for Kids!*** Here's what you will find inside:

- fascinating **facts** you won't believe
- entertaining **stories** to share
- cool **activities** to test your skills
- easy and delicious **recipes** to try
- amazing **tales** of kids' accomplishments
- challenging **games**
- garden **ideas** to get you growing
- useful **information** that you'll remember for a lifetime

We hope that you enjoy every word on every page—and we'd love to know if you do (or don't)! Send us your thoughts, opinions, ideas, and impressions at **Almanac.com/feedback.** Or mail a letter to ***The Old Farmer's Almanac for Kids,* P.O. Box 520, Dublin, NH 03444.** Thanks for buying this book. We want the next one to be even better!

NOW, TURN THE PAGE AND LET THE FUN BEGIN!

The Almanac Editors

CONTENTS

CALENDAR

ASTRONOMY

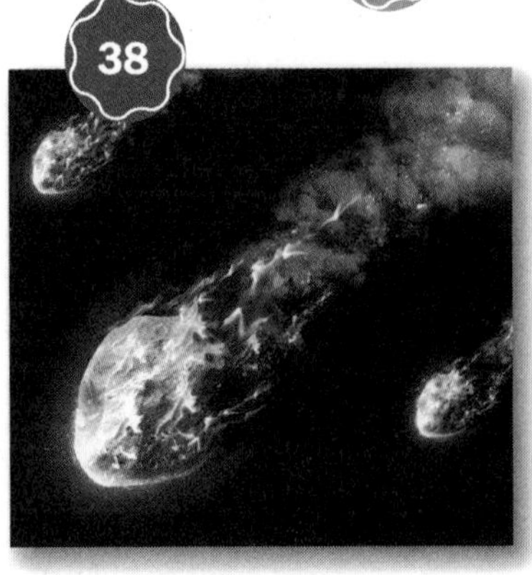

WEATHER

IN THE GARDEN

NATURE

HEALTH

CONTENTS

HISTORY

FOOD

PETS

SPORTS

AMUSEMENT

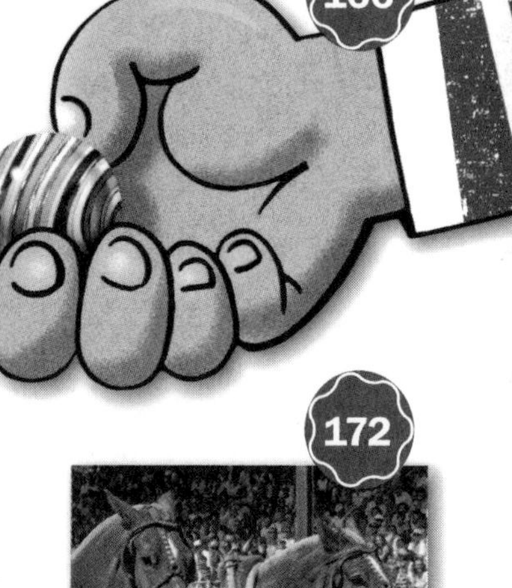

172

Make EVERY

You don't need an occasion to celebrate, recreate, investigate, officiate, cogitate, or captivate—special days proliferate! Here are some uncommon events on otherwise ordinary days of the year. Pick a date—don't hesitate! Or get some friends and collaborate.

JANUARY

International Brain Teaser Month

Put your noggin to the test! Ponder these cranial conundrums until you crack them! (Answers below.)

1. Why are some letters above the line and some below?

A E F H I K L M N T V W X Y Z

B C D G J O P Q R S U

2. Use four 9s in a math equation that equals 100.

3. You need to take a fox, a chicken, and some corn across a river in a boat. But it's a small boat that will hold only you and one other thing. If you take the fox and leave the chicken with the corn, the chicken will eat the corn. If you take the corn and leave the fox with the chicken, the fox will eat the chicken. How do you get the fox, the chicken, and corn across the river in the fewest trips?

Answers: 1. "Straight" letters are above the line and "curvy" letters are below. 2. 99 + (9/9) = 100. 3. Take the chicken across the river and leave it there. Return across the river alone. Take the fox to the other side. Leave the fox and return with the chicken. Leave the chicken and go across with the corn. Leave the corn and the fox and go back alone. Finally, take the chicken across again and join the fox with the corn.

DAY Special

A B C D E F G H I J K L M

N O P Q R S T U V W X Y Z

● = raised

JANUARY 4 LOUIS BRAILLE'S BIRTHDAY

On this day in 1809, Louis Braille was born near Paris, France. At age 3, he punctured his eye with his father's shoemaking tool. Infection set in and then spread to the other eye, leaving Louis blind.

In 1829, he first published his system of raised dots (the Braille alphabet), which enabled sight-impaired people to read by feeling them.

TRY THIS! "Write" in Braille, using small-dot stickers. Indicate "on" and "off" on a light switch plate; put your name on your lunch box; or compose a message to a friend.

JANUARY/FEBRUARY

BALD EAGLE APPRECIATION DAYS

Bald eagles live in every state except Hawaii and in all provinces of Canada. Sightings are frequent in midwinter because the eagles fly over open waters and countryside in search of food. Many communities celebrate these magnificent creatures with educational programs and group viewing events.

Research more about the bald eagle: Why is it called "bald" if it has feathers? When and why did it become the official symbol of the United States?

TRY THIS! Create a bird guide booklet about the bald eagle, listing fun facts about it such as size, diet, range, speed, population, behavior, and habitat.

FEBRUARY

NATIONAL BIRD-FEEDING MONTH

As seed heads on plants get depleted, our feathered friends need us to help them get their nourishment. Here's a seed wreath that is fun and easy to make.

Convert to metric on p. 181

YOU WILL NEED:

- ½ cup warm water
- 1 package unflavored gelatin
- 3 tablespoons light corn syrup
- ¾ cup all-purpose flour
- 4 cups bird food (seeds, peanuts, berries, dried fruit)
- Bundt pan or other mold
- nonstick cooking spray

1. Put the warm water into a large bowl. Add gelatin and stir until dissolved. Add corn syrup and flour. Whisk until there are no lumps. Add the bird food. Stir well. (If not mixed well, the wreath could fall apart.) The mixture will be very sticky.

2. Spray the Bundt pan or mold with nonstick cooking spray. Pour the bird food mixture into the pan. Press it down evenly and set aside overnight.

3. When ready, the wreath will be hard and white. If it is soft, set it aside for a few hours more. Turn over the mold to release the wreath. Tie a ribbon on it and hang it for the birds to feast on.

FEBRUARY 5

WEATHERPERSON'S DAY

On this day, John Jeffries was born in Boston in 1744. One of America's first weather observers, in 1784 he made the first flight over London in a hot air balloon, on which he carried weather instruments as well as greeting cards, which he dropped to onlookers. Jeffries kept detailed weather records in Boston from 1774 until March 1776 and from 1790 to 1816. Prized as authentic climatic data, these are stored at the Blue Hill (Mass.) Meteorological Observatory.

TRY THIS!

Keep a weather diary for 1 month. Each day, go to almanac.com/weather, enter your zip or postal code, and get the forecast. Record it. Then record the weather outside your window. Calculate a percentage to express how accurate the forecasts were.

WORLD RADIO DAY

Radio was the first wireless form of communication using electricity. In 1895, 21-year-old Guglielmo Marconi devised what he called "the wireless telegraph"—the instrument we now call radio. Radio works by changing sounds or signals into radio waves that travel through air, space, and solid objects to a receiver that changes them into the sounds, words, and music we hear.

TRY THIS!

Find an old radio. Turn it on and switch between AM and FM stations. What differences do you detect in reception? In programming?

Visit a radio station and meet the staff. Interview them about their jobs, their listeners, and the future they see for radio.

Create a 15-minute audio show on something about which you are curious. Find and interview an expert. Develop a beginning and end, with sound effects or music. Edit the segments. Gather friends and family to listen.

FEBRUARY 18 PLUTO DISCOVERY DAY

On this day in 1930, astronomer Clyde Tombaugh peered through a telescope lens at the Lowell Observatory in Flagstaff, Arizona, and discovered what he thought was the ninth planet of the solar system. It was given the name of the Roman god of the underworld—Pluto.

TRY THIS!

RESEARCH what happened to this "planet."

CREATE a model of the solar system. Provide background information on the discovery and naming of all of the planets.

MARCH

Youth Art Month

Show off and celebrate your creativity and that of your friends!

- Make edible art, using fruit and vegetables, or bake and decorate a cake.
- Walk the chalk: Decorate your sidewalk or driveway.
- Paint faces at lunch.
- Organize a school art show, then take it on the road for display in a grocery store, town hall, senior center, or other public space. For the show, dress as your favorite artist or piece of art.
- Visit an art museum or artist's studio.

MARCH 2

HI TO HIGHWAY NUMBERS

On this day in 1925, a government board was appointed to create a numbering system for U.S. Numbered Highways (e.g., U.S. Route 66). In 1956, the Interstate numbering system (e.g., I-95) was added. In general . . .

- North–South routes take odd numbers. U.S. Route numbers increase from east to west; Interstates, the opposite.
- East–West routes take even numbers. U.S. Route numbers increase from north to south; Interstates, the opposite.

ROUTE
US
66

Find a fun fact about each of the 10 longest roadways in the world. Use the information to create a match game. See how well your friends and family do on your quiz.

MARCH 18

JOHNNY APPLESEED DAY

On this day in 1845, John Chapman, also known as Johnny Appleseed because he planted so many apple trees, died. Born in Massachusetts on Sept. 26, 1774, Chapman owned more than 1,000 acres of farmland on which he grew apple trees and other plants. Every year, he traveled hundreds of miles on foot sharing seedlings, seeds, and fruit.

MAKE YOUR OWN DRIED APPLES

YOU WILL NEED:

kitchen knife
apples
1 quart water
¼ cup lemon juice

Convert to metric on p. 181

1. Preheat oven to 115°F. Wash, peel, and core some apples. Cut the apples into slices about ¼-inch thick. Rinse them in 1 quart water mixed with ¼ cup lemon juice (to keep the apples from turning brown).

2. Place the slices in a single layer on an ungreased cookie sheet. Bake for 3 to 4 hours. Turn the slices over and bake for another 3 to 4 hours. Cool and enjoy as snacks.

EARLY MARCH

GENEALOGY DAY

Genealogy is the study of family lineage.

TRY THIS!

Create a family tree with the names of your family: your grandparents and any aunts, uncles, and first cousins. Add photos, if available. Note births, marriages, and deaths, along with historic events.

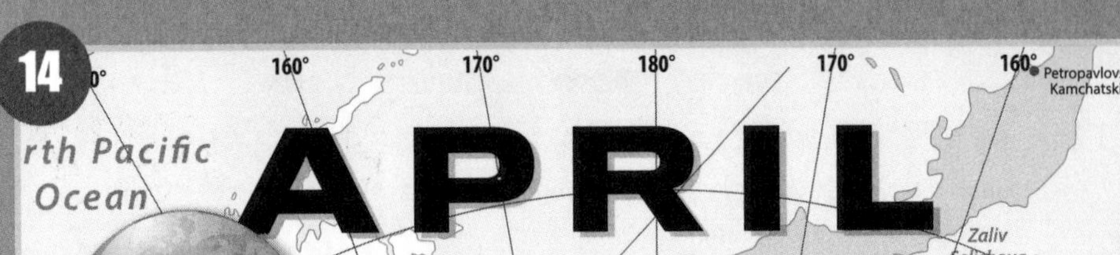

APRIL

GEOGRAPHY BEES

Around April 1, *National Geographic* state geography bees are held in every state and the District of Columbia. How would you do?

TRY THIS!

Answer these questions from national bees of the recent past. (Answers below.)

1. Mariupol, a city at the mouth of the Kalmius River, is located on what sea that is an arm of the Black Sea?

2. Helsignor's strategic location on a narrow strait allowed Danish kings to collect tolls from passing ships. Name the strait.

3. A Russian island that straddles 180 degrees longitude is one of the most biodiverse in the Arctic and is the world's northernmost UNESCO World Heritage Site. Name the island.

4. The Strait of Canso separates mainland Canada from what island?

5. Name the landlocked country that borders Botswana and South Africa.

6. The Milan Cathedral lies in the valley of Italy's longest river. Name the river.

7. Which state has two panhandles?

8. Lake Superior borders Michigan, Minnesota, and which other state, Missouri or Wisconsin?

9. Which state produces more peanuts: Georgia or Utah?

Answers: 1. Sea of Azov. 2. Øresund. 3. Wrangel Island. 4. Cape Breton Island. 5. Zimbabwe. 6. Po River. 7. West Virginia. 8. Wisconsin. 9. Georgia

GLOBAL YOUTH SERVICE DAY

This is the largest volunteer event in the world, celebrated in more than 100 countries. Get involved!

TRY THIS!

ORGANIZE a "trash mob"—like a flash mob, it's a "race" to pick up trash for a specific time (30 minutes) in a single location.

RECRUIT friends to read with or tutor younger students.

BUILD a school garden that can provide fruit and vegetables for school meals or a community food bank.

INVITE an exchange student to share a meal or stay for a weekend with your family.

APRIL 23

World Book Day and Night

These celebrations of reading were founded in 1995 and 2011, respectively. World Book Day is for kids; World Book Night is for adults. A few things to do:

TRY THIS!

MEET with reluctant readers and others wanting recommendations for a good book.

MAKE comics or mini-books based on your favorite story.

PLAN with friends to each put your favorite literary quotes on a T-shirt. Challenge each other to find out who said it and in what book.

MAKE bookmarks that relate to books or authors that are special to you. Distribute them to family and friends.

MAY

NATIONAL SWEET VIDALIA ONION MONTH

Vidalia onions are sweet. They are very low in sulfuric acid (the juice in yellow onions that makes your eyes tear). Vidalias are named for the area in which they grow—around Vidalia, Georgia.

TRY THIS!

GET a Vidalia onion and a yellow onion. Cut up each one and see the effect that it has on your eyes. Use the chopped Vidalia onion in a sandwich or salad. Use the yellow onion for cooking. Try it on a pizza.

GROW onions—it's easy! Onion "sets" are available in spring. (Onions can be grown from seed, but this requires a lot more time.) Set the bulbs, root end down (not pointed end down), 1 inch deep in soil that drains well and gets sunlight all day. Water regularly and watch for its green shoots to appear. Pull your onions out of the ground when the shoots dry out. Set the onions aside in a cool, dry place (not a refrigerator), away from apples and potatoes.

RESEARCH the different types of onions. Make a chart showing each one's specific characteristics.

Convert to metric on p. 181

1st FULL WEEK

NATIONAL PET WEEK

Pets enrich our lives with companionship, humor, love, and affecton. Not just cats and dogs, but birds, fish, gerbils, rabbits, and more really are our best friends!

MAY 17

James "Cool Papa" Bell was born on this day in 1903. He played in baseball's "Negro leagues" for 25 seasons, from 1922 to 1946. "Cool Papa" had a career batting average of .338, and he was regarded as the fastest man ever to play the game: He could round the bases in 12 seconds. Bell was inducted into the Baseball Hall of Fame in 1974 and died in 1991.

TRY THIS!

- Read biographies of other sports heroes who also overcame prejudice, such as Jackie Robinson, Jesse Owens, Wilma Rudolph, Althea Gibson, and Hank Aaron.
- If you can not travel to the Baseball Hall of Fame, take a virtual tour on its Web site (baseballhall.org).
- Write a rhythmic cheer or song for a game or sport that doesn't usually have cheerleaders (baseball, chess, weightlifting, golf, or tennis).

AROUND MAY 18

International Museum Day

Museums are an important means of cultural exchanges and enrichment, as well as platforms for the development of understanding and peace among people.

MAKE plans to go to a museum that you have never visited. Research in advance; many museums are free on this day and/or offer special programs.

INQUIRE at your local library about free passes to museums in your area. (Many libraries offer passes that can be reserved for use by patrons.)

TRY THIS!

Do something special for animals:

VOLUNTEER at a local animal shelter. Tasks often range from walking the animals to cleaning cages to talking to them.

INVITE a veterinarian to talk to your class about his/her job, how to care for a variety of animals, and how to become a vet. Or ask your librarian to arrange such a program.

CLEAN your pet's bed, pen, house, tank, cage, or whatever is its "private" space.

J•U•N•E

SUPERMAN DEBUTS

JUNE 1

In 1938, Superman first appeared in a comic book—Action Comics #1 (June). He was created by teenage science fiction enthusiasts and friends Joe Shuster and Jerry Siegel. Jerry "dreamed up" much of Clark Kent's looks and personality; he actually woke up from his sleep and wrote notes.

TRY THIS!

DRAW a comic strip of someone you consider to be heroic—your parents, a sibling, a teacher, an aunt or uncle, a friend, or a figment of your imagination. Give him or her exaggerated strengths (and weaknesses) in real-life situations.

CREATE a comic strip based on a character from one of your favorite books. Change the book's story line in your comic: Have the characters act differently.

JUNE 5

United Nations World Environment Day

World Environment Day began in 1972 as a time for all of us to do something to take care of Earth. The "something" can be local, national, or global; by yourself or in a group or crowd; and of any size or scope. Here are some ideas:

- Set aside an area of your garden where you can experiment with decomposition times. Choose items that you'd like to compare, such as paper, orange peels, a piece of milk carton, and a plastic bag. Bury the items in the garden about 4 inches deep. Use craft sticks to mark what you buried where. Every 2 weeks, dig up an item to see whether it has decomposed. Write a science project report about your findings.
- Make something useful out of your trash:
  - Make jewelry out of pull tabs or bottle caps.
  - Start seeds in margarine or yogurt tubs.
  - Use old sheets and towels as rags for cleaning the car or your bicycle.
  - Make a skirt or tote bag out of an old pair of jeans or other clothing.

2nd WEEKEND IN JUNE

Banana Split Festival

Since 1995, attendees at this event in Wilmington, Ohio, have piled scoops of ice cream, whipped cream, sweet sauce, nuts (maybe), and a cherry on top of sliced (split) bananas—and eaten it all! Wilmington claims that its citizen E. R. Hazard invented the banana split in 1907.

TRY THIS!

- Research which other cities claim to be the place where banana splits were invented. Make a list of the differences in the situations and split ingredients.
- Make a banana split! Here are the traditional ingredients; use other flavors, if you prefer.

FOR EACH SPLIT, YOU WILL NEED:

1 scoop each vanilla, chocolate, and strawberry ice cream
3 to 4 tablespoons each pineapple, chocolate, and strawberry sauce
1 banana, peeled and cut lengthwise
whipped cream
chopped nuts (optional)
1 to 3 maraschino cherries

Convert to metric on p. 181

Put the ice cream into a boatlike dish. Top each scoop with a sauce, in the order given. Place the banana slices alongside the ice cream. Top with whipped cream, nuts (if using), and cherries.

4th SATURDAY

GREAT AMERICAN BACKYARD CAMPOUT

Today's the opening event of a summerlong celebration of connecting with nature and wildlife. Plan to pitch a tent tonight and sleep out!

MAKE a list of the equipment and supplies that you would need to camp out for one night. What would change if you were to camp out for two nights?

WORK with a parent, teacher, or community leader to arrange a public campout in a park or other open space, so that kids without a backyard can participate.

WRITE a journal about your campout experience. Include the weather; items packed; notes on setting up and breaking down (packing up) camp; sights and sounds; explorations; and ways in which being outdoors is different from being indoors.

JULY

JULY 3

On this day in 1608, French explorer Samuel de Champlain founded a settlement called "Québec." The name comes from the Algonquian word *kébec,* which means "where the river narrows." Quebec City is one of the oldest communities of European origin in North America.

- Create a map of Canada, with all of the provinces and territories and their capital cities.
- Canada has at least 46 national parks. Identify five and make a list of each one's distinctive characteristics (location, origin, size, features, and fun facts). Add them to your map.

JULY 10 CLERIHEW DAY

Edmund Clerihew Bentley (1875–1956) was a British journalist with a keen sense of humor. He invented the four-line poem about a person named in it, in which the first two lines rhyme and the last two lines rhyme, usually comically. He called the verse a "baseless biography," and it has become known as the "clerihew," named for him.

Here's a clerihew by Bentley . . .

Sir Humphrey Davy
Abominated gravy.
He lived in the odium
Of having discovered sodium.

. . . and another:

It only irritated Brahms
To tickle him under the arms.
What really helped him to compose
Was to be stroked on the nose.

TRY THIS!

WRITE a clerihew about one of your parents, a friend, or a character in history, in a book, on a TV show, or in sports.

TELL your teacher about the clerihew. Work with your teacher to make writing them a class project, with kids sharing their verses.

JULY 20

"ONE GIANT STEP FOR A MAN . . ."

On this day in 1969 at 4:17 P.M. EDT, astronauts Neil Alden Armstrong and Edwin Eugene Aldrin Jr. made mankind's first landing on the Moon in the lunar module *Eagle.* They remained on the lunar surface for 21 hours, 36 minutes. Their colleague, Michael Collins, remained aboard the orbiting command module, *Columbia.*

- Visit the Web site live.slooh.com and explore outer space through its telescopes, especially on full Moon nights. (The Web site is free but membership is required. Get help from a parent or teacher.)

LAST FULL WEEK IN JULY (FOR 9 DAYS)

NATIONAL MOTH WEEK

Calling "moth-ers" of all ages: Celebrate the beauty, life cycles, and habitats of moths! Observe, learn about, and document these fascinating creatures. To observe moths easily, leave a porch light on after dark.

TRY THIS!

MAKE moth bait: Mix up a banana, stale beer, and a couple of spoonfuls of brown sugar. Put it aside to ferment for a few days. Using a paintbrush, apply patches of bait about chest high on trees along a path or at the edge of a field or other property. Wait a few hours. After the Sun sets, go out with a flashlight and check the bait spots. Record what you see!

RESEARCH the differences between a moth and a butterfly. Compare them through their life cycles.

August

1st SATURDAY

National Mustard Day

Ancient Greeks and Romans consumed mustard as a paste and powder. Today, we eat more than 700 million pounds of mustard each year worldwide. There are three types of mustard: yellow, which is used as a condiment and as dry mustard, and brown and oriental, which are used for oil and spices. Some mustards are grown for their edible leaves, while others are grown for seeds.

- Tendergreen mustard is a leafy vegetable also known as komatsuna, named for a district in Japan in which it grows abundantly. It is like spinach and easy to grow. Get some seeds. Ask an adult to help you prepare a garden or pot of soil with compost. Plant the seeds about 6 inches apart. Water regularly. Leaves are ready to harvest in about 40 days. Pick them and eat in a salad or stir-fry.

TRY THIS!

Make Honey Mustard

YOU WILL NEED:

½ cup ground mustard
⅓ cup white vinegar
¼ cup honey, or to taste
pinch of salt

Convert to metric on p. 181

Ask an adult for help. Put the mustard, vinegar, honey, and salt into a saucepan and stir to combine. Cook over medium heat for 3 to 5 minutes, or until the mixture thickens slightly. Remove from the pan. Cool to room temperature. Serve. Store any that remains in a glass jar. *Makes about 1 cup.*

AUGUST 7

NATIONAL LIGHTHOUSE DAY

This day was first observed in 1989 to mark a 1789 law establishing federal lighthouses.

TRY THIS!

- Research the oldest original lighthouse in service, the only triangular lighthouse, the tallest lighthouse, the first lighthouse to use electricity, and/or the only lighthouse with an elevator.
- Read about life in a lighthouse. You might try *The Lighthouse Keeper* by James Michael Pratt; *Lighthouse Girl* by Dianne Wolfer; or *Lighthouses of North America! Exploring Their History, Lore, and Science* by Lisa Trumbauer.

- If possible, visit a lighthouse.

AUGUST 8

Matthew Henson Born on This Day in 1866

Matthew Henson was the first African-American Arctic explorer—and so much more. At age 11, an orphan, he left his home in Washington, D.C., and walked to Baltimore to get a job as a cabin boy on a three-masted ship. Years later, while working at a hat shop in Washington, D.C., he met explorer Robert Peary and began 22 years of travel, discovery, and adventure.

READ Matthew Henson's autobiography, *A Negro Explorer at the North Pole.*

After reading his book, WRITE a pretend letter to Matthew Henson about what you learned from his life story.

RESEARCH to compare climate and living conditions in the Arctic when Henson and Peary traveled there with those conditions today.

AUGUST 16

National Roller Coaster Day

In 1878, Richard Knudsen was awarded a patent for the first wooden roller coaster. It consisted of a four-passenger car that ran on two wooden tracks between two towers. Gravity caused the car to roll down the tracks; a lift mechanism hauled it up. Alas, Knudsen never built his "inclined-plane railway."

TRY THIS!

RESEARCH who built the first roller coaster, also known as the "gravity pleasure ride." Write a profile of the man and the ride.

CREATE a chart distinguishing the differences between the steepest, fastest, tallest, longest, and oldest operating roller coasters in the world.

SEPTEMBER

NATIONAL HONEY MONTH

- Honey is one of Mother Nature's sweeteners. Use it as syrup on pancakes or ice cream.
- Try it as a natural home remedy . . .

Got chapped lips? Rub honey on them and leave it there overnight.
Got a sore throat? Drink warm lemon tea sweetened with honey.

- Give yourself a facial: Spread honey over your face and leave for 10 minutes. Wash away with warm water. The honey tightens pores just as well as expensive facial masks do.
- Define these bee terms: apiculture, apis, beekeeper, colony, comb, drone, hive, honey, nectar, pollen, queen, and worker. Make a word search or crossword puzzle with the words. Give your puzzle to a friend to solve.

SEPTEMBER 1

First Book of Poetry by an African-American Published

Phillis Wheatley's *Poems on Various Subjects, Religious and Moral* came out on this day in 1773, becoming the first printed book of poetry composed by an African-American.

- Research Wheatley's life and create a timeline, beginning with her arrival in America as a slave. Note other famous historic events that took place in her lifetime, including the Boston Tea Party.
- The first known African-American poet was Lucy Terry Prince. Only one of her poems survives. It is "Bars Fight," a description of a Native American raid on the village of Deerfield, Massachusetts. Research Lucy Terry Prince and compare her life with that of Phillis Wheatley.

"OLD IRONSIDES" PUBLISHED

On this day in 1830, a newspaper in Boston published "Old Ironsides" about the USS *Constitution*, one of the country's first battleships. Oliver Wendell Holmes wrote the verse when he learned that Congress had voted to scrap it. Numerous other newspapers also ran the poem. Citizens read it, and they too demanded that "Old Ironsides" be saved. Today, it is the oldest U.S. commissioned vessel afloat.

TRY THIS!

- Research why the USS *Constitution* was called "Old Ironsides."
- Find other U.S. naval ships with well-known nicknames. Choose one, research its history, and write a poem about it.
- Visit ussconstitutionmuseum.org and explore the online exhibits. Like history? Look at the scrapbooks compiled by members of the crew between 1931 and 1934.

OLD IRONSIDES

By Oliver Wendell Holmes

Ay, tear her tattered ensign down!
Long has it waved on high,
And many an eye has danced to see
That banner in the sky;
Beneath it rung the battle shout,
And burst the cannon's roar; —
The meteor of the ocean air
Shall sweep the clouds no more!

Her deck, once red with heroes' blood,
Where knelt the vanquished foe,
When winds were hurrying o'er the flood
And waves were white below,
No more shall feel the victor's tread,
Or know the conquered knee; —
The harpies of the shore shall pluck
The eagle of the sea!

Oh, better that her shattered hulk
Should sink beneath the wave;
Her thunders shook the mighty deep,
And there should be her grave;
Nail to the mast her holy flag,
Set every thread-bare sail,
And give her to the god of storms, —
The lightning and the gale!

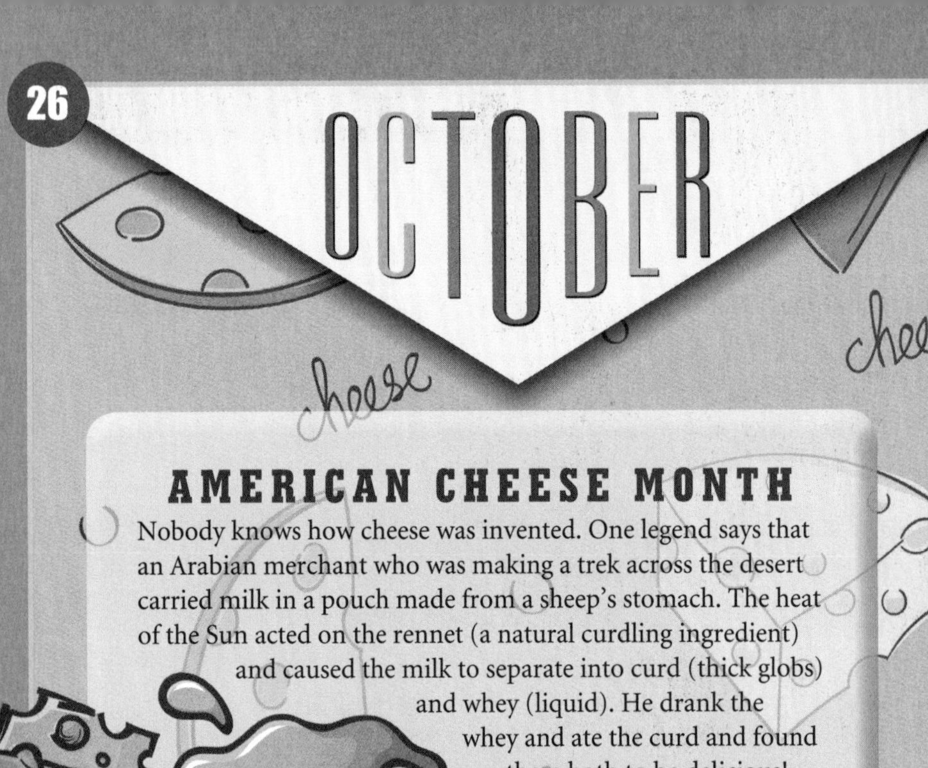

AMERICAN CHEESE MONTH

Nobody knows how cheese was invented. One legend says that an Arabian merchant who was making a trek across the desert carried milk in a pouch made from a sheep's stomach. The heat of the Sun acted on the rennet (a natural curdling ingredient) and caused the milk to separate into curd (thick globs) and whey (liquid). He drank the whey and ate the curd and found them both to be delicious! Some ancient Roman homes had a room, called a *careale,* used only for making cheese. In the 16th century, cheese was used as money by some people. England's Queen Victoria received a 1,000-pound wheel of cheddar cheese for a wedding gift (a "normal" wheel of cheddar weighs 60 to 75 pounds). In 1993, Crayola named one of its crayon colors "Macaroni and Cheese." More than one-third of all milk produced in the United States is used to make cheese. There are more than 2,000 varieties of cheese. Macaroni and cheese has been a favorite comfort food for centuries. President Thomas Jefferson served it to friends. The most popular cheese used to make it is cheddar.

Convert to metric on p. 181

NATIONAL ROLLER-SKATING MONTH

What has four wheels, two feet, and lots of laughs? A kid on roller skates! Roller-skating has been around since the 1760s.

TRY THIS!

VISIT rollerskatingmuseum.com to learn quirky facts about the sport through the years.

ASK an adult to visit kidsskatefree.com. Find the roller-skating rink nearest you. Join the Web site (for free) and follow the guidance to get two free passes for up to four kids.

RESEARCH the health benefits of roller-skating.

NATIONAL MOLE DAY

Calling chemists of all ages! Join in a commemoration of Amedeo Avogadro's Number (6.02×10^{23}) that takes place from 6:02 in the morning until 6:02 in the evening (get it?). Avogadro was born in Turin, Italy, on August 9, 1776. In 1811, he proposed that equal volumes of gases, at the same temperature and pressure, have the same number of molecules. This explains why a balloon inflates when you blow air into it, why a flat tire gets larger when it is pumped up, and even why our lungs expand when we breathe: Gas molecules are being forced into each object. Why call today National Mole Day? Because Avogadro's idea resulted in a unit of measure called a "mole."

- The Mole Day mascot is the mammal that lives underground. Research and report on the life of a mole.
- Craft a mole from fabric or other soft goods. Be creative: Give it personality!

NOVEMBER

NOVEMBER 2

ON THIS DAY IN 2000, at 5:23 A.M. EST, astronauts for the first time docked with and boarded the International Space Station (ISS). The crew, dubbed Expedition 1 by NASA, consisted of American commander Bill Shepherd and Russian cosmonauts Sergei Krikalev and Yuri Gidzenko. Launched from central Asia in a Russian Soyuz space shuttle, they stayed for 137 days, conducting experiments and making the facility more livable.

Today, the ISS can hold a crew of six. More than an acre of solar arrays provides power. Research more about the International Space Station:

- How high above Earth is it? How many crews have lived there? What is the record number of days an astronaut has lived on the ISS?
- The ISS travels at 5 miles per second and orbits Earth every 90 minutes. Watch it fly over: Go to spotthestation.nasa.gov for guidance.

THE BIRTH OF THE SANDWICH

On this day in 1718, John Montagu was born into an aristocratic family in England. At age 11, he became the fourth Earl of Sandwich, inheriting the title from his grandfather. Two things got their name from his: the meal that consists of two slices of bread with filling between them and an island chain.

- The sandwich took its name from Montagu when, in 1762, he spent 24 hours playing cards and eating only meat between two slices of bread. He was considered a daring man for eating with his fingers!
- English explorer Captain James Cook named the Sandwich Islands after Montagu in 1778. We now know these islands as Hawaii.

TRY THIS!

SALUTE THE EARL OF SANDWICH WITH CHOCOLATE PEPPERMINT SANDWICH COOKIES

YOU WILL NEED:

Cookies:

1½ cups all-purpose flour
½ plus ⅛ teaspoon baking soda
¼ teaspoon salt
6 tablespoons butter
¾ cup brown sugar
6 ounces semisweet chocolate chips
1 egg

Filling:

1½ cups confectioners' sugar
2¾ tablespoons butter, softened
⅛ teaspoon peppermint extract, or to taste
2 tablespoons milk

Convert to metric on p. 181

Preheat oven to 350°F. Lightly grease two baking sheets.

For cookies: In a bowl, sift together flour, baking soda, and salt.

Put the butter, brown sugar, and 2 tablespoons of water into a saucepan over low heat. Stir as the butter melts. Add chocolate chips, stirring as they melt. Remove from heat and let cool. Add egg and beat to blend. Pour into flour mixture and stir to combine.

Drop by heaping spoonfuls onto the prepared baking sheets. Bake for 8 to 10 minutes, or until edges are dry but centers are still soft. Transfer to a rack to cool.

For filling: In a bowl, combine all ingredients and beat until smooth. Spread 1 spoonful of filling on one cookie. Top with another cookie.

Makes about 18 sandwich cookies.

FRIDAY AFTER THANKSGIVING

Native American Heritage Day

Celebrate the culture and traditions of Native Americans.

Make a cornhusk doll. To Native Americans, these figures are spiritual messengers spreading brotherhood and contentment. These dolls traditionally have no face because, according to legend, the first cornhusk person was so beautiful that she became conceited.

YOU WILL NEED:
several dried inner cornhusks
string
glue (optional)
corn silk (optional)
scissors

1. Soak the dried cornhusks in warm water to soften.
2. *For the head:* Make a ball with a cornhusk. Fold two cornhusks over the ball and tie off the neck with string.
3. *For arms:* Roll one or two husks into a tight tube and tie off the ends. Or roll three husks separately and braid them. Tie off the ends.
4. *For the body:* Position the arms under the neck. Fold husks over each shoulder and cross them below the arms. Tie string at the midpoint (the waist).
5. *For hair (optional):* Smear glue on the head and attach corn silk.
6. Trim the cornhusks a few inches below the waist so that the doll will stand up.

NOVEMBER 29 LOUISA MAY ALCOTT BORN

On this day in 1832, Louisa May Alcott was born in Germantown, Pennsylvania. In 1849, her family moved to Concord, Massachusetts. She wrote many stories but gained fame in 1869 with her book *Little Women,* based on her memory of her own childhood, about four young sisters: Meg, Jo, Beth, and Amy. The success of the book enabled her to pay off her family's debts. Books that followed included *Little Men* and *Jo's Boys.*

READ *Little Women* or *Jo's Boys.* Write a story about you and one of the characters.

GO to Concord, Massachusetts, and visit the Alcotts' home, Orchard House. Or go to louisamayalcott.org to see it and "tour" the rooms on screen.

DECEMBER

DECEMBER 5

UNITED NATIONS WORLD SOIL DAY

Good soil is essential for growing fruit, vegetables, flowers, trees, grass, and more! Today is dedicated to raising awareness of why soil is necessary for life.

Soil can be sour (or acidic) or just right (neutral) or sweet (alkaline). This quality is expressed as a "pH" number on a scale of 0.0 (acidic) to 14.0 (alkaline). Soil pH affects plant production and health.

TRY THIS!

- Get a soil test kit at a local plant nursery or home goods store and test your soil's pH.
- Go to almanac.com/content/ph-preferences. Based on your soil test results, make a list of the plants that would grow best and worst in your soil.
- Research how to change soil pH—how to make sour soil sweeter and sweet soil more sour.

DECEMBER 21 OR 22

WINTER SOLSTICE

This marks the shortest day (and longest night) of the year and the beginning of winter in the Northern Hemisphere. The word "solstice" comes from the Latin words *sol*, which means "sun," and *stitium*, which means "stoppage."

- Research why this happens (hint: Earth is tilted).
- Research how this day is different in the Southern Hemisphere.
- Many people celebrate with bonfires. Make solstice lanterns to welcome daylight's return.

YOU WILL NEED:
paper or plastic cups
scissors or knife
markers (optional)
colored paper (optional)
glue (optional)
hole punch
flameless electric tea lights

1. Ask an adult to help cut off the cups' bottoms. Discard them. Decorate the cups with markers or colored paper.

2. Use the punch to make holes around the sides of the cups. Punch holes in a pattern or randomly.

3. Switch on the tea lights and place the cups over them. Welcome the light!

Tricks to Remember How Many Days in THE MONTHS

A DITTY OF DAYS

No one knows who wrote this little verse, which has been traced back to the 15th century. We do know that in the mid-1880s, C. F. Springman, headmaster of the Royal Jubilee School in Newcastle-on-Tyne, England, used rhyming words and poems to help his students remember facts. His most famous lesson still helps kids and adults to keep track of the number of days in each month. Many slightly different versions exist today, but this is one of the easiest. Say it five times, and you'll never forget it:

Thirty days hath September,
April, June, and November;
All the rest have thirty-one,
Except poor February alone.

KNUCKLES OF KNOWLEDGE

If you can't remember the verse or how many days are in each month, knuckle down and try this:

- Make a fist with each hand. Put your fists together, side by side, thumb and first finger touching.
- Beginning with the knuckle of the baby finger on your left hand, count out the months on your knuckles and the valleys in between.

All of the knuckle months have 31 days. The valleys are short months; February is the shortest. How short? 28 days, except for Leap Years, when it has 29 days.

January is the baby finger knuckle.

February is the valley between your baby finger and ring finger knuckle.

March is the ring finger knuckle.

The next valley is April.

The middle-finger knuckle is May.

June is the next valley.

July is the knuckle on your pointer finger.

Skip your thumb knuckles and valleys.

August is the knuckle of the pointer finger on your right hand.

September is the next valley.

October is the next knuckle, the one on your middle finger.

The next valley is November.

December is the knuckle on your right-hand ring finger.

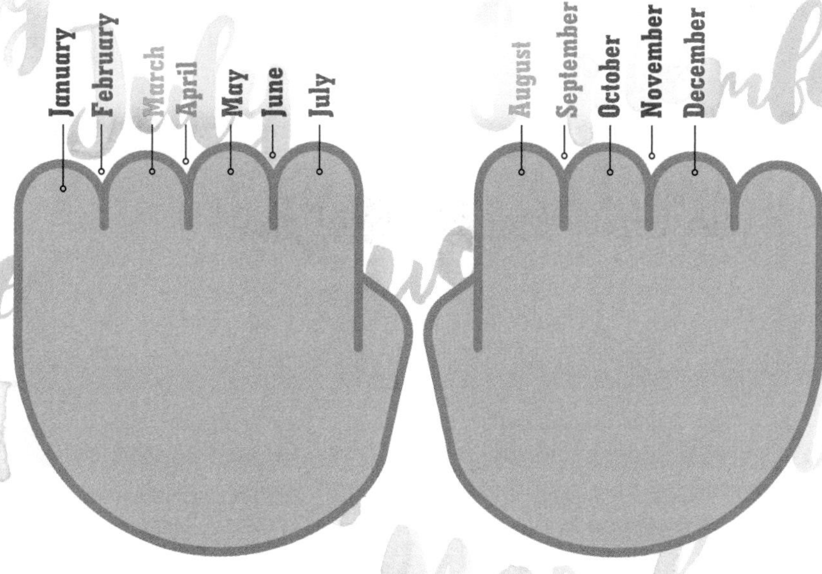

SPRINGTIME FUN AROUND THE WORLD

In many places, the transition from one season to the next is an occasion for a party. The changes from winter to spring, and eventually summer, signal a fresh start; warmer, longer days; the new growing season; and even time to vacation. Through the centuries, people have celebrated with customs that you might find unusual, but read on: These festivities are also a lot of fun!

SADDLE UP

Every Easter Monday in Traunstein, Germany, men and women don festive attire and decorate horses for a historic procession in honor of St. George, patron saint of farmers and horses. Bands play, blessings are bestowed, and sword dances are performed to symbolize the victory of spring over winter. Thousands of people come out to watch the horseback parade, a tradition dating back to the 18th century.

SPLASH AND DASH

The Easter Monday Polish tradition is a water fight called *Śmigus Dyngus* (SHMEE-goose DING-goose). Traditionally, men and boys can throw water on unmarried women and girls or wet them with squirt guns. To avoid a dousing, a girl may offer the boy a decorated egg. An ancient folk custom associated with the end of winter and beginning of the growing cycle, the dousing is considered a symbolic cleansing. Fair play is encouraged: The next day, women and girls get to douse the men and boys!

SPOT THAT POT

On the day before Easter Sunday in Greece, bells ring, bands parade through the streets, and people throw clay pots out of windows, smashing them on the ground. (Of course, they do this when nobody is going to get hurt!) A practice since the 16th century, the ritual symbolizes the death of evil spirits and the return of light and new life to the world.

CATCH THEM IF YOU CAN

In old England, the seventh Sunday after Easter marked the beginning of summer. Celebrations date back to the 12th century, when King John allowed the people to use the fields and collect wood for burning. Bread and cheese were blessed and tossed to the poor in St. Briavels parish; today, the tradition continues with townsfolk using umbrellas to catch the offerings, now considered to be lucky charms.

CLEAN, SHOP, AND SHARE

In Iran, the first day of spring (and the beginning of the Iranian or Persian new year) is called *Nowruz* (NO-rooz), meaning New Day. Preparations include spring-cleaning, the buying of new clothes, and preparing special foods. On the last Wednesday before Nowruz, bonfires are lit and both young and old jump over the flames, in hope of good health in the new year. On Nowruz, families and friends exchange gifts and feast. They spend the 13th day of the new year and last day of celebrations outdoors, believing that bad luck comes to those who stay inside on this day.

Color festival at Sri Sri Radha Krishna Temple in Spanish Fork, Utah

COLOR THE WORLD

In late February or early March (the date depends on the Full Moon) in India, Nepal, and countries with large Hindu populations, spring is welcomed with “Happy Holi” greetings. Holi is the Festival of Colors or Festival of Love. The night before the festival, people gather around bonfires to sing and dance. On the day of the festival, friendships are renewed; old hurts discarded; water and bright-color, perfumed powders tossed on the crowds; and colored powders rubbed on faces, spreading fun and merriment everywhere.

Open Your Eyes and

A meteor or shooting (or falling) star begins to form when a chunk of rock breaks off from an asteroid or comet. The comet or the asteroid then releases a trail of dust and rocks that hurtle freely through space. Each of these rocks is called a meteoroid, and 10 or so of these enter Earth's atmosphere haphazardly every second.

On its way through the atmosphere, a meteor heats up drastically,

Catch a Falling Star

Ready a front-row seat to pure spectacle and ground-breaking events!

creating the streak of light that briefly appears in the sky on a dark, clear night and occasionally during the day.

Usually, because of the intense heat and friction, a meteor will disintegrate before it ever reaches the ground. However, if one lands, it then is called a meteorite. Meteorites are rare finds. For this reason, they have become collectors' items, and, depending on their type, they can be very valuable.

COMING ATTRACTIONS

Several times a year, Earth passes through a cloud of debris left by an asteroid or comet. This causes many meteoroids (small bodies of matter in the solar system that become meteors if they enter Earth's atmosphere) to enter the atmosphere in a relatively short period of time. We call this flurry a meteor shower.

Meteor showers vary in size, and some are easier to see than others, but because the orbit of Earth is always the same, there are a few showers that occur at the same time each year. There are 12 annual meteor showers, but three are known to be the brightest and most visible:

- QUADRANTID—peak: around January 4. Frequency: averages 25 meteors per hour. Best time to watch: before dawn.
- PERSEID—peak: around August 11–13. Frequency: averages 50 meteors per hour. Best time to watch: the predawn hours.
- GEMINID—peak: around December 13–14. Frequency: averages 75 meteors per hour. Best time to watch: throughout the night.

Convert to metric on p. 181

SHOWER PARTY POOPERS

- Cloudy skies can prevent you from seeing a meteor shower.
- The Moon, too, can interfere: On nights when it is full or close to full, lunar light can wash out your view.

The best shower shows occur when the Moon is new or close to new and the sky is clear.

THE FALLING STAR

I saw a star slide
down the sky,
Blinding the north
as it went by,
Too burning and
too quick to hold,
Too lovely to be
bought or sold,
Good only to make
wishes on
And then forever
to be gone.

–Sara Teasdale,
American poet
(1884–1933)

THE WORLD'S MOST EXPENSIVE MAILBOX

In 1984, the mailbox belonging to the Barnard family of Claxton, Georgia, was hit by a 3-pound meteorite traveling at 300 miles per hour. The mailbox was completely ruined, but the Barnards were more than repaid for the inconvenience when that very mailbox sold for nearly $83,000 at an auction in 2007.

A REALLY BIG SHOW

On November 27, 1872, a storm of meteors from Comet Biela appeared to radiate from near the constellation Andromeda—and that's how this shower got its name: Andromedid. People in China described seeing it as stars falling like rain, and Italian observers recorded about 85 meteors per hour. A less intense (50 meteors per hour) Andromedid shower occurred on the same day in 1885.

Then the Andromedids disappeared . . . until December 3–5, 2011, when they fell at a rate of about 50 per hour.

Guess what: They're coming back for two shows, and one will be bigger than ever!

- In 2018, the Andromedids are expected to appear at a rate of 35 meteors per hour.
- In 2023, they are predicted to light up the sky with up to 200 meteors per hour.

Both Andromedid meteor showers are expected to occur on November 25–27, but they could happen in early December. These showers are at their most active during the late evening.

ATTENTION: NEW ASTEROID IN YOUR ORBIT

A recently discovered small asteroid named 2016 HO3 is being called a quasi-satellite of Earth. This means that while orbiting the Sun, 2016 HO3 also circles our planet, in the same way that a man-made satellite orbits Earth. It is estimated to have been following this pattern for over a century and is expected to be around for several more.

In the recent past, only one other asteroid—2003 YN107—has followed a similar orbital pattern, but it is no longer in our vicinity.

MAMMOTHS AMONG US

Most meteorites are small enough to hold in one hand. However, sometimes a larger meteor will make it through the atmosphere and down to Earth. The largest meteorite on record in the United States was found in a wheat field in Nebraska in 1948. Many witnesses who saw the fireball (the name often given to extremely bright meteors) fall to Earth said that it appeared brighter than the Sun. The meteorite was found buried 10 feet deep in the ground and weighed 2,360 pounds.

When large meteorites strike Earth, the impact caused by their speed and mass often creates a crater: a big, bowl-shape hole in the ground, usually with a rim around the perimeter. The largest crater ever created by a meteorite is Meteor Crater in Arizona. The hole is 600 feet deep and a mile wide, with a rim that rises 150 feet. The meteorite that created this immense cavity roughly 50,000 years ago is estimated to have been about 150 feet across and traveling at 26,000 miles per hour.

Convert to metric on p. 181

IT'S NEW! IT'S OLD! IT'S AMAZING!

Recently, a new type of meteorite was found in Thorsberg, Sweden. The roughly 3-inch rock was given the name Österplana 65. Scientists found that it had broken off from its parent asteroid about 470 million years ago, at the same time that another, larger class of meteorites called the L chondrites had broken off from their parent. This suggests that the two were broken off as a result of the same collision, but the Österplana 65 has distinct oxygen and chromium signatures indicating that it could not be from the same asteroid as the L chondrites. For this reason, scientists believe that this new meteorite came from the second asteroid involved in this collision. Although the impact of the hit likely broke off more than just this single space rock, some are now referring to the Österplana 65 as an extinct meteorite, as other rocks of its kind are likely to be found only in fossil sediments.

LEARN THE LINGO

- **METEOROID:** a piece of icy, metallic, or stony matter that breaks off from an asteroid or comet and hurtles freely through space. Most are fairly small, usually not exceeding the size of a boulder.
- **METEOR:** a meteoroid that enters Earth's atmosphere, creating a streak of light across the sky that is visible on a dark, clear night.
- **METEORITE:** a rare (and usually small) meteor that does not disintegrate entirely on its way through the atmosphere, resulting in only a portion of it making its way to the ground.
- **COMET:** a giant, frozen ball of rocks, gases, and dust that, when heated by the Sun, has a glowing head and a long tail made from the material that spews from its melting exterior.
- **ASTEROID:** a space rock that is similar to planets and moons in material, but much smaller in size. Nevertheless, some asteroids are big enough to be considered dwarf planets or even to have their own moons!

MAKE A METEORITE MAGNET

You just might find a meteorite! Attach a magnet to the end of a broomstick, then wander around waving your magnet on or just above the ground. Meteorites contain a lot of iron, so if you come across one, it will stick to the magnet. Of course, some regular old rocks contain iron and will attach themselves as well. You can tell a meteorite from a rock by its thin, glassy coating called a fusion crust, which was formed from the extreme heat that occurred during the meteorite's fall through the atmosphere.

METEOR MEANINGS

Throughout history, Native Americans have held spiritual beliefs about meteors and meteor showers.

- The Cahuilla of southern California believed that a meteor was the spirit of their first shaman, Takwich. He was said to wander the night sky, looking for people who had left the safety of the tribe. When he found them, he would steal their soul or eat them alive.
- The Chumash of coastal California believed that meteors were souls traveling to the afterlife.
- To the Blackfeet of Montana, a meteor shower meant that the tribe would be sick in the coming winter or that their chief had just died.
- The Shawnee in Ohio, West Virginia, South Carolina, and Oklahoma believed that meteors were living beings, running from danger or a threat.
- Many tribes, including the Nunamiut of Alaska, the Koasati of Louisiana, and several in southern California, thought that meteors were star "poop."

LEGENDS AND LORE

- In Switzerland, a meteor was thought to possess the power of God.
- In England, it was often said that a shooting star represented the soul of a newborn baby.
- Many Romanian peasants believed that stars were candles, that a star formed every time someone was born, and that when he or she died, the star's light went out as a meteor.
- Centuries ago, people in southern Germany believed that seeing one shooting star signified a year of good fortune to come. However, anyone who saw three in one night was doomed to die prematurely.
- For good luck, Filipinos seeing a shooting star would tie a knot in a handkerchief before the meteor disappeared.

STAR LIGHT, HOW BRIGHT?

Star brightness is called magnitude. The lower the magnitude number, the brighter the star. On a clear night, away from city lights and with binoculars, we can see stars that are a magnitude +6 or +7. On a clear night in a city or suburb, we can see stars of magnitude +2, +3, or +4 with the naked eye. Here are some relative examples:

YOU CAN SEE . . .	MAGNITUDE	WITH . . .
Sun	−26	proper eye protection (never look at the Sun without it)
full Moon	−13	naked eye
crescent Moon	−6	naked eye
Venus	−4	naked eye
Jupiter	−2	naked eye
Sirius (star)	−1	naked eye
Vega (star)	0	naked eye
Saturn	+1	naked eye (best in dark, rural areas)
Big Dipper (stars)	+2	naked eye
Andromeda Galaxy	+3 or +4	naked eye
moons of Jupiter	+5	binoculars
Uranus	+6	binoculars
bright asteroids	+7	binoculars
Neptune	+8	telescope
some comets	+10 to +13	telescope
Pluto, at its brightest	+14	telescope

SUPERSTAR TEENS

Make History

These kids discovered objects in deep space just by looking!

At age 14, Caroline Moore, from Warwick, New York, made her first major astronomical discovery as part of a research team led by astronomer Tim Puckett in Atlanta, Georgia, in 2008. She found a supernova in the galaxy named UGC 12682, making her the youngest person to have ever discovered a supernova. After studying it, scientists determined that Caroline's supernova is the weakest on record, being 1,000 times weaker than the typical supernova. Caroline got her first telescope when she was 10 years old. She now has 10 telescopes. She followed her passion for astronomy and now works with the telescope development company Celestron.

A SUPERNOVA

is a star exploding at the end of its life cycle. The power of its explosion is measured and compared by calculating how much light was given off at the moment of explosion and the speed at which the explosion was able to launch matter through space.

In 2012, high school students Cecilia McGough (from Virginia) and De'Shang Ray (from Maryland) were participants in a summer Pulsar Search Collaboratory (PSC) workshop. During the program, they announced their discovery of the pulsar with the widest orbit ever seen in its category. This colossal discovery has helped astronomers to better understand star systems and how they evolve. After high school, each pursued a science degree: Cecilia studied astronomy and astrophysics at Pennsylvania State University, and De'Shang studied biology, engineering, and emergency medical service at the Community College of Baltimore County.

A PULSAR

is a rapidly spinning neutron star. It can also be the extremely dense remains of stars that have exploded as a supernova. While it spins, a pulsar emits lighthouse-like beams of radio waves that, when passing by Earth, can be detected by radio telescopes.

At age 7, Tom Wagg got his first telescope. In 2013, when he was 15 years old, he spent a week studying data from an international space program as a part of an astrophysics course at Keele University in England. He spotted evidence of a dip in the brightness of a star. After some investigation, he discovered that the dip indicated that something was passing in front of the star. The "thing" was an undiscovered planet! Located in our galaxy 1,000 light-years away, the planet is roughly the size of Jupiter and named WASP-142b. Tom became the youngest person to discover a planet. Today he attributes his accomplishment to luck, saying that no matter the skills of an astronomer, it is rare to actually make a discovery of this significance.

A PLANET

is a spherical object that orbits a star and is big enough to pull smaller objects into itself or move them out of the way with its gravity.

TEENAGE GALAXIES
Shine a Light on Stars

Like people, galaxies change with time. They are born, grow, and eventually reach adulthood, or full maturity—and this occurs over hundreds of thousands to billions of years! In childhood, galaxies grow by consuming flows of gas. This enables them to form new stars. As adults, galaxies consume other smaller galaxies and their stars instead of forming new ones.

In recent years, scientists have learned about galaxies' middle years—their "teens."

In 2012, a camera with ultraviolet light sensitivity was installed on the Hubble Telescope. The camera allows astronomers to observe galaxies between the childhood and adult stages. We now know that the teenage galaxies have a heavier concentration of stars and matter near their outer edges, unlike the older galaxies, which have the highest concentration closer to their center. That's not all: Astronomers are now able to see the brightest, youngest stars that are forming within these teenage galaxies and are learning more about how stars take their ultimate shape. As astronomers collect more information from this camera, we will continue to better understand how galaxies age.

WHAT IS A GALAXY?

The Milky Way is one. Andromeda is another. Scientists can not agree on a definition but conclude that a galaxy is a collection of stars and mysterious dark matter with other particular characteristics. That's why they are studying teen galaxies!

WHO WAS Hubble?

In the 1920s, Edwin Hubble used the largest telescope of that time to observe galaxies beyond our own from the observatory atop Mt. Wilson in California. Eventually, he developed the theory that the universe is ever-expanding.

Seventy years later, a new telescope named for this passionate astronomer became the first of its kind to be launched into space. The telescope is the length of a large school bus and orbits Earth at 17,000 miles per hour. During its more than 25 years of use, it has made upward of 1.2 million observations of the universe, without ever leaving Earth's orbit.

Convert to metric on p. 181

GET YOUR EYES On the Sky!

Here are a few ideas to help you enjoy the night sky. You might discover something, too!

- Find a naturally dark spot, where artificial light does not intrude when night skies are clear of clouds. Having a telescope or binoculars is helpful, but you can see a lot with the naked eye. Observe and write down or draw what you see.
- With an adult, go to almanac.com/astronomy to help you identify the constellations and planets that appear in the night sky.
- Visit public observatories and planetariums to learn more.
- Start an astronomy club at school. Ask a science teacher to help, recruit members, and then plan fun projects that will help you to deepen your knowledge of space. Reach out to other local astronomy clubs to share equipment, ideas, and discoveries.

MYTHS ABOUT THE MOON

What do you think of when you look at the Moon? For centuries, people have imagined characters and events to help them understand the Moon's presence and its phases. Here is a collection of mythical Moon stories from around the world.

The Incas of Peru called their beautiful Moon goddess Mama Quilla. She cried tears of silver. They believed that lunar eclipses were caused by an animal or serpent attacking Mama Quilla. Whenever one occurred, the Incas would try to scare it away by making as much noise as possible.

In Finnish mythology, Ilmatar, the daughter of the air, allowed a duck to lay its eggs on her knee. The eggs fell, and their whites became the Moon, their yolks became the Sun, and tiny fragments of their shells transformed into stars.

The Babylonian Moon god, Sin, had a beard of lapis lazuli (a deep blue gemstone) and rode a winged bull. He represented the number 30, which is the average number of days in a lunar month.

In Greek mythology, the Moon goddess Selene, sister of Helios, the Sun, drives a silver chariot drawn by two snow-white horses across the sky each night.

One Amazonian tribal myth says that when time began, there were so many birds that they blocked out all light shining on Earth. Two heroic brothers, Iae and Kuat, captured the king of the birds and forced him to share the light. Iae became the god of the Moon and Kuat, the god of the Sun.

In Polynesian myths, Hina was an accomplished young woman pursued by many men. She fled to the Moon and became its goddess and the protector of travelers at night.

In India, the Moon's waxing and waning phases are explained by a story about the Moon god Chandra, who was cursed by his father-in-law, Daksha, to shrink in size to nothing. The major god Shiva intervened, instead causing Chandra to diminish in size for 15 days, but then grow back to his normal size for 15 days—and repeat the pattern forever.

The Japanese Moon god, Tsukuyomi, was born from a mirror made of white copper. He climbed a ladder into the heavens, where he lived with his sister, Amaterasu, the goddess of the Sun.

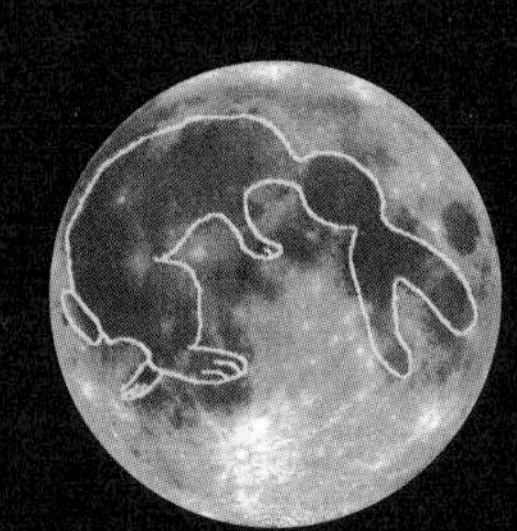

The Mayas of Central America believed that the Moon was the mother of the Sun, who was a young boy pestered by his elder siblings. She caught one of the elder brothers and turned him into a rabbit, whose image can be seen in the full Moon.

A Dozen Meteorological Mysteries

WEIRD, WILD, AND SCARY WEATHER EVENTS EXPLAINED

WEATHER

JANUARY 2015

The Case of the Snowless Snowmobiles

In January 2015, the Seven Clans International 500-Mile Snowmobile Race from Winnipeg, Manitoba, to Wilmar, Minnesota, was called off because there was no snow on the ground. The race, with 350 to 400 entrants, dates from the 1960s. This was not the first time that lack of snow was a problem. The event was canceled for 2 years in the 1980s. Race director Brian Nelson said, "If anything, there will be more enthusiasm for it next year."

Despite the enthusiasm, the snow stayed away and the 2016 race was also canceled. El Niño, the warm Pacific Ocean current, reduced snowfall in both winters.

Convert to metric on p. 181

FEBRUARY 2015

THE CASE OF THE MILKY RAIN

On February 6, 2015, people in parts of Washington, Oregon, and Idaho found their cars and windows covered with a grayish powder left by a rainstorm. Meteorologists who collected the rain noted that it was "milky" in color and that it might contain ash from volcanoes in Russia or Mexico.

This didn't make sense to other scientists. The volcanoes were thousands of miles away, and the wind that brought the milky rain had come from a different direction. Closer analysis showed that it was high in sodium, the main element in salt. This led investigators to Oregon's Summer Lake, a shallow body of water that often dries up during droughts.

The night before the mysterious rain, Summer Lake had winds of up to 60 miles per hour, strong enough to lift a cloud of sodium-rich dust into the atmosphere and carry it 480 miles to the affected region.

MARCH 2015

THE CASE OF THE MISSING STORMS

The national Storm Prediction Center (SPC) regularly posts an online map showing all thunderstorm and tornado watches across the continental United States. From March 1 to 24, 2015, the map was blank. This was the first time that this had happened in the 45 years that the SPC had been keeping records. Although March is not normally a big month for tornadoes, an average of 78 twisters touch down in the month.

Experts believe that abnormally cold, dry weather in the central United States prevented any outbreaks in March of that year.

APRIL 2011

The Case of the Swarming Storms

In 2011, 303 tornado warnings were issued on one day, April 27, when a combination of moisture from recent thunderstorms, warm air from Mexico, and cold air from Canada created ideal conditions for tornadoes in the central and southern United States, especially Alabama and Mississippi.

Later, some scientists suggested that smoke from huge fires in Central America might also have played a part in the situation, which produced one of the largest, costliest, and deadliest tornado outbreaks in U.S. history. The fires' black soot drifted northeast and settled over the southern United States, trapping the Sun's heat and creating wind patterns that often produce tornadoes.

MAY 1780

THE CASE OF THE DARK DAY

In the midday hours of May 19, 1780, night birds began to sing and people had to light candles in order to work and do chores. Some frightened folks thought that it was the end of the world. Although the darkness was deepest in Maine and northeast Massachusetts, as far south as New Jersey, Gen. George Washington reported in his diary seeing dark clouds "and at the same time a bright and reddish light intermixed with them, brightening and darkening alternately."

The event came to be known as New England's "Dark Day."

Since then, scientists have proved that the darkness was caused by smoke from burning forests in Canada. The crucial evidence came from charcoal found in tree rings dating to that month in 1780.

JUNE 1816

The Case of the Disappearing Summer

Six inches of snow in Vermont in June is unusual, but not unheard of. Usually it melts and is forgotten. But in 1816, the cold weather lasted all summer. Frosts killed crops, and people—and animals—went hungry. Many Vermonters gave up on New England and moved west and south to warmer areas.

Scientists think that the unusually cold weather was caused by an event that happened a year earlier on the other side of the world—the eruption of Mt. Tambora, in what is now Indonesia. The huge explosion shot enough ashes and dust into the atmosphere to put the entire Northern Hemisphere into the shade. The period is now famously known as "The Year Without a Summer."

JULY 1843

The Case of the Flying Alligator

"The beast had a look of wonder and bewilderment about him, that showed plainly enough he must have gone through a remarkable experience." So reported the editor of the *Charleston Mercury* of a 2-foot-long alligator found at the corner of Wentworth and Anson streets on the morning after a terrible thunderstorm that rocked the South Carolina city on July 1, 1843.

Small animals falling like rain have been reported for hundreds of years. Most experts believe that the creatures are sucked into the sky by strong updrafts of wind or even tornadic waterspouts that form over oceans and lakes and then carry them long distances before they fall to Earth.

Convert to metric on p. 181

AUGUST 2014

THE CASE OF THE SLIDING STONES

A part of California's Death Valley is called Racetrack Playa (*playa* is Spanish for "beach") because of the mysterious tracks in the sand left by large, heavy stones.

Scientists solved the mystery in August 2014, after having witnessed stones being moved hundreds of feet across the desert in 2013 and 2014. The sliding stones are embedded in or pushed by thin sheets of ice that in turn are propelled by the wind along an even thinner layer of meltwater. The combination of ice, water, and mud is slippery enough to allow even heavy stones to move in light winds. The ice forms because in Death Valley nighttime temperatures can fall below freezing.

SEPTEMBER 1995

The Case of the Monster Wave

The navigation bridge of the *Queen Elizabeth 2* stands about 100 feet above the surface of the sea. So imagine how Captain Ronald Warwick felt at 4:00 A.M. on September 11, 1995, when he saw dead ahead a wave whose crest was at his eye level. "It looked as though the ship was heading straight for the White Cliffs of Dover [England]," he said.

He had already altered course to avoid Hurricane Luis, which was creating winds of 130 miles per hour and kicking up enormous waves. But the monster he saw before him was no ordinary wave, and his ship was about to hit it.

"An incredible shudder went through the ship, followed a few minutes later by two smaller shudders. There seemed to be two waves in succession as the ship fell into the 'hole' behind the first one," he reported. "The second wave crashed over the foredeck, carrying away the forward whistle mast."

The monster was a "rogue wave," produced by the multiplying effect of many waves in perfect synchronization. Fortunately, damage to the ship was slight and no passengers or crew were injured.

OCTOBER 1962

THE CASE OF THE WILDEST WINDS

It's hard to say exactly how strong the winds of the 1962 Columbus Day Storm were. On this day, October 12, the weather station in Corvallis, Oregon, measured a gust of 127 mph just before the anemometer (the instrument for measuring wind speed)—and the tower it was attached to—was blown down and destroyed. Also blown down were countless trees, many of which were more than 1,000 years old. Buildings suffered, too: Of the 4,000 structures in the town of Lake Oswego alone, 70 percent were damaged.

The unusual storm developed when the remnants of Typhoon Freda combined with a powerful storm off northern California and raced northward with little warning. Scientists called it an "extratropical cyclone," meaning a hurricanelike storm that develops outside the tropic zones. In the Pacific Northwest, survivors just called it the Big Blow.

NOVEMBER 1933

THE CASE OF THE BLACK BLIZZARDS

On November 11, 1933, high winds blew an enormous cloud of dust into the atmosphere, obscuring the Sun and burying farms in the Great Plains under as much as 6 feet of loose dust. The dust blew from South Dakota to New England, where it turned snowflakes red.

Eventually, 100 million acres of farmland were affected, and hundreds of thousands of farmers had to move out of the area.

Most historians date the beginning of the Dust Bowl to this day. Scientists believe that it may have been directly caused by changes in ocean currents in the Pacific Ocean, but it was also due to overcultivation, new technology (mechanical tractors and harvesters), and a misunderstanding of the limits of natural resources like topsoil and water.

Convert to metric on p. 181

DECEMBER 2008

The Case of the Shattering Trees

On the night of December 10–11, 2008, millions of people in New England were awakened by the terrifying explosive crash of tree limbs breaking and falling, the boom of whole trees toppling, and the thunder of heavy chunks of ice smashing into and cascading onto their roofs.

Everything was coated with ½ to 1 inch of ice. The trees, and miles of power lines, were brought down by the weight of it. Households were robbed of electric power for up to 2 weeks, and many schools were closed until January 2009.

A rare combination of unusual warmth the day before, a sudden invasion of freezing or below-freezing air from Canada, and a strong moist airflow from the south had caused heavy rain that coated every surface and froze.

Weather's

A LITTLE GIRL'S POEM ABOUT SNOW

Charley boy looked at the snowflakes fair,
Falling so swiftly through the air.
With wonder in his big blue eyes
He looked at the fairies from far-off skies.
Soon he called, "Mamma, come look at these things,
Floating as softly as if they had wings.
I guess, Mamma, the angels up there
Are combing the dandruff out of their hair!"

–Cora E. Talbot, American composer (1865–1938)

Pleasures

COUNTING THE RAINDROPS

Rain! Rain! Rain! coming from the sky—
Drip, drip, drip, on children passing by.
Can you count the raindrops, Carrie,
If upon the way you tarry? . . .
Now, Lucy, count the drops of rain—
They travel on a lightning train.
Their numbers you must quickly say—
For lazy counting they won't stay.
See how they run and rush and hurry!
Helter, skelter! Hurry, scurry! . . .
Now, thicker, faster, down they come!
Millions of raindrops from their home
In the Cloudland, up so high.
Do you think the raindrops die
When down to the earth they fall?
"Yes," you say? Oh, not at all!
Watch them closely, and you'll see
they're very fond of company.
They run together in a band
When they safely reach the land.
They do not like alone to stay;
They never say, "You shall not play."
Each little drop says to the other,
"Come, sister, quick! Run, hurry, brother!
The more the merrier," they say.
"There's better sport where many play."
Billions and trillions join the sport,
And not one baby drop is hurt.

–Ellen T. Sullivan (c. 1890)

SIGNS OF CHANGE

For centuries, mankind has attempted to predict the weather. Here are some of the ways.

WHAT THE HEAVENS FORETOLD

- Ancient Egyptians rejoiced each year when heavy rain caused the Nile River to flood. The waters deposited rich soil for crops. The people predicted the flood by watching for the star Sirius (which they called "Sothis"). The floods came as the star started to rise just before the Sun in the morning. (This was a coincidence.)
- **Early Greeks and Romans believed that the star Sirius and the Sun shining together brought hot, unhealthy weather in midsummer. Sirius, which is in the constellation Canis Major, or "Greater Dog," was also called the Dog Star. The ancients called the hot spell the "dog days." (We do, too.)**
- Comets were said to forecast cold weather.
- **Bright northern lights foretold a storm.**
- Twinkling stars could mean rain or snow soon.
- **Halos around the Sun, Moon, or a planet could indicate wind, rain, or snow.**
- The color and shape of the Moon also signaled a change. People made up rhymes to help them remember. For example . . .
  The Moon, her face if red be,
  Of water speaks she.

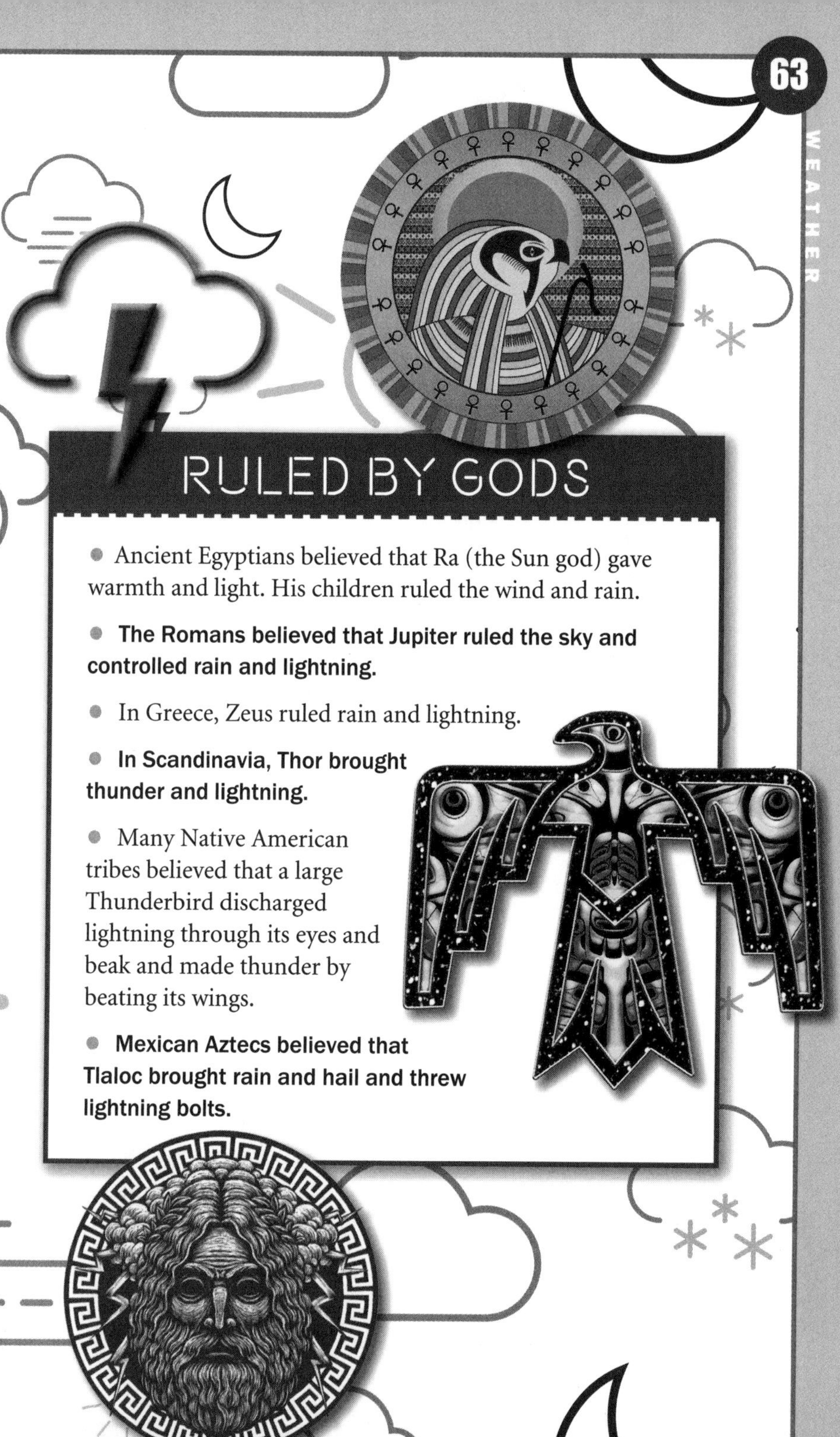

RULED BY GODS

- Ancient Egyptians believed that Ra (the Sun god) gave warmth and light. His children ruled the wind and rain.
- **The Romans believed that Jupiter ruled the sky and controlled rain and lightning.**
- In Greece, Zeus ruled rain and lightning.
- **In Scandinavia, Thor brought thunder and lightning.**
- Many Native American tribes believed that a large Thunderbird discharged lightning through its eyes and beak and made thunder by beating its wings.
- **Mexican Aztecs believed that Tlaloc brought rain and hail and threw lightning bolts.**

DID YOU KNOW?
In appreciation of good weather or to request a change, some ancient peoples sacrificed animals. Several Native American tribes performed dances, especially when they needed rain.

CLOUD COVER

- As early as 650 B.C., Babylonians were looking to clouds to predict the weather. In the centuries since then, lots of folks have studied cloud patterns, shapes, colors, heights, and more. They have also created rhymes and sayings to help them remember:

Mackerel clouds in sky,
Expect more wet than dry.

The higher the clouds, the finer the weather.

- Our ancestors knew that a cloudless day after a storm often heralds another storm within 24 hours. They called the clear period a "weather breeder."

ANIMAL AND PLANT OMENS

• Farmers predicted weather by studying nature. They devised sayings or poems expressing their observations, such as . . .

When pigs carry sticks,
The clouds will play tricks;
When they lie in the mud,
No fears of a flood.

If bees stay at home,
Rain will soon come;
If they fly away,
Fine will be the day.

• Farmers also made predictions based on animal body parts. For example, if a goose bone (left over from dinner) turned blue, rain was expected.

• Plants have long signaled weather conditions. Some flowers close before rain falls, and some tree leaves expose their undersides when a storm approaches. People believed that even onions could predict the coming winter and came up with this verse:

Onion's skin very thin,
Mild winter's coming in;
Onion's skin thick and tough,
Coming winter cold and rough.

DID YOU KNOW?
To American colonists, creaky chairs, clumped salt, and smoke that descended to the ground all meant rain.

SICKLY SYMPTOMS

- Ringing ears indicated a change of wind direction.
- **Rain was expected if injuries started to ache or corns itched more than usual.**
- Poor digestion was said to occur before a storm.
- **A bad dream would be taken as a bad omen heralding a change in weather.**

DID YOU KNOW?
In the 4th century B.C., Greek philosopher Aristotle and his student Theophrastus of Eresus wrote about the weather. Experts consulted their work for nearly 2,000 years.

MODERN METEOROLOGY

- Over time, people began to record and compile their weather observations and invented tools to help them with research. From the 14th through 17th centuries, scientists devised instruments to monitor moisture, temperature, air pressure, wind speed, and other aspects of weather.
- **With the invention of the telegraph in the mid-1800s, weather observations and predications could be shared over greater distances. This improved scientists' understanding of large weather systems.**
- Using collected records and data, people learned how winds and storms moved.
- **Starting in 1929, scientists launched radiosondes—boxes with weather instruments and a radio transmitter—into the atmosphere. Today, weather balloons are launched every 12 hours from hundreds of weather stations around the world. Data from them are used to construct weather maps and models to help with predictions. Meteorologists now also use satellites, which provide images and data about the atmosphere around the globe.**
- Weather remains unpredictable at times—enough so that it is worthwhile to observe plants, animals, and the sky for recurring patterns, just as our ancestors did.

The STORIES THESE GARDEN GOODIES COULD TELL!

Some vegetables have had adventures on their way to your plate. Remember this the next time you have them!

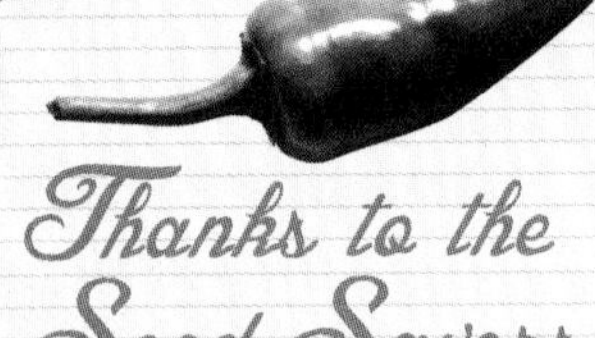

Thanks to the Seed Savers

Over centuries, vegetable seeds have been carried around the world by immigrants, slaves, refugees, missionaries, soldiers, and explorers. They smuggled seeds sewn into a hem, stashed inside the lining of a suitcase, hidden under a hat band or in a hollow cane, or concealed under a postage stamp—all so that they could grow and eat the food they loved.

BRUSSELS SPROUTS

From the 5th to 15th centuries, *spruiten* (Dutch for sprouts) were grown in large quantities in Belgium. The capital of Belgium is Brussels . . . so soon this vegetable had a new name. The first report about brussels sprouts as we know them was written in 1587, and interest in this new food spread rapidly throughout Europe. Germans called a sprout a *rosenkohl,* or "rose cabbage," because it resembles a rosebud.

In August 2014, a British man named Stuart Kettell pushed a brussels sprout (actually 22 of them) up Mount Snowdon in Wales with his nose–all to raise money for cancer.

CELERY

In 628 B.C., Selinunt, Sicily, was the celery capital of the world. (*Selinon* is the Greek word for celery.) Celery was used as a flavoring and medicinal herb, and coins were embossed with its leaves. Ancient Romans wore crowns of celery leaves to avoid headaches. Later, medieval magicians believed that putting celery seeds into their shoes would enable them to fly!

Kalamazoo, Michigan, was once called "Celeryville" because a lot of celery was grown there.

Celery grows best in damp, marshy areas. The sweetest stalks result from blanching—piling soil around them as they grow.

Chinese Cabbage

The Chinese have cultivated Chinese, or Napa, cabbage for centuries. Many cabbage varieties are called Chinese cabbage, but some are originally from Thailand. During the 18th century, European missionaries in China brought seeds home, and interest in the plant spread.

Legend has it that around 1900, the Chinese empress fell ill with fever, constipation, low energy, and difficulty breathing. A monk recommended that she consume only Chinese cabbage juice and soup—and she recovered.

Cucumber

Some 4,000 years ago, cucumbers were discovered growing wild in India. As people found them pleasing, their popularity spread throughout the Middle East and southern Europe. Ancient Romans loved cukes and built greenhouses just for growing them. Emperor Tiberius ate one every day!

Christopher Columbus introduced cucumbers to the Caribbean islands. Native Americans learned of them from European hunters.

In the 1700s, in England, somebody started the rumor that cucumbers were poisonous and best used as cow feed, so they were then called "cowcumbers." By 1836, "no well-taught person" called them this, and people everywhere ate and enjoyed them as "cucumbers."

EGGPLANT

For centuries, eggplant has grown wild and been cultivated in Southeast Asia and India, where it is called the King of Vegetables. British colonists there named it, based on its shape. For centuries, artists have painted and drawn eggplants' many shapes, and cultures have celebrated it in the folklore:

- In Turkey, the south wind is the "eggplant wind" because it blows on the fires on which eggplants are grilled.
- In Sicily, eggplant's name in Italian means "partridge" because cooks cut it to look like wings.
- In Japan, on New Year's Day, people say that the happiest omen is first Mount Fuji, then the falcon, and then the eggplant.

NEW ZEALAND SPINACH

New Zealand spinach is not a true spinach, but it is native to that island nation. Luckily, Sir Joseph Banks discovered the plant growing on the shores of Queen Charlotte's Sound during Captain Cook's voyage in 1770. It proved to be a valuable source of vitamin C for the sailors and was introduced in North America soon after.

The plant is sometimes called summer spinach. Its small, triangular leaf does not look like spinach, but it has a similar taste.

POTATO

The Incas of Peru were growing potatoes as early as 8000 B.C. Today, we have more than 4,000 international varieties—one for almost every ethnic group, including 'Russian Banana', 'Swedish Peanut', 'Irish Cobbler', 'Rose Finn Apple', and 'Purple Peruvian'. The German 'Lady Finger' potato, brought to North America by immigrants, is called a fingerling because it resembles a human finger.

Thomas Jefferson first served french fries in America. They were cut in rounds and curlicues.

In October 1995, potatoes aboard the Space Shuttle *Columbia* became the first vegetables to be grown in space.

Convert to metric on p. 181

Sunchoke

The name "Jerusalem artichoke" comes from the Italian *girasole articiocco,* meaning "sunflower artichoke," but the plant is not from Israel (it is native to North America) and it is not an artichoke! It is related to the sunflower and, like it, turns its blossoms toward the Sun.

In 1615, French explorer Samuel de Champlain noticed the 6- to 10-foot-tall plants being grown by Huron Native Americans. He collected samples and brought them to France, where people loved it.

Today, this vegetable is often called a sunchoke. The edible portion is its potato-like tubers that grow underground. Any tuber or piece of one that is not lifted from the soil will sprout a new plant in the next growing year.

TOMATO

The Aztecs, natives of Mexico, discovered and cultivated the tomato, which they called the *tomatl,* meaning "plump fruit." Spanish explorers brought it home to Spain, and before long, people all over Europe were eating it. A Dutchman claimed that it made people feel romantic, earning it the nickname "love apple."

In 1692, Italians wrote down the recipe for tomato sauce, and folks have been spreading the love ever since—that is, except for a few years when some people thought that the tomato was poisonous, in part because its leaves sometimes stink.

WELCOME FAIRIES!

When you invite sprites, magical things happen.

Do you believe in fairies? These pixielike creatures with playful personalities, dressed in beautiful, flowing, pastel-color clothing, happily soaring through the air on silky, butterfly-like wings, have been with us for centuries. If you accept them, they feed your imagination and creativity.

- Fairies are shy, sensitive beings who can be seen only by people who believe in them. They live in a magical place where time runs differently, and they never grow old.
- Fairies love to sing, dance, listen to music, and have parties at midnight. They occasionally move or hide people's belongings in the garden for their own amusement.
- Fairies take care of our environment. Every plant—whether tree, shrub, flower, or even weed!—has a fairy to protect and take care of it.
- Fairies wear sparkly accessories and decorations, and their favorite food is sweets, such as candies, cakes, and cookies—one piece at a time.
- Fairies appreciate respectful children, especially when they laugh, smile, play, dance, splash, paint, or do whatever makes them happy.

SHOW FAIRIES LOVE AND FRIENDSHIP

To welcome fairies, create a special place for them and be careful about where it is. A good spot would be at the base of a tree, on a tree stump, under a bush, near a birdbath, or nestled beneath a big leaf. Fairies need protection from frisky pets and kids playing or people walking about.

Your special fairy space need not be out of sight, but it must be safe.

Give the fairies a house or a portion of one. You could collect twigs and glue them together to form a small structure. Or get an unfinished wooden birdhouse, paint it with bright colors, and glue on pinecone scales as siding and craft sticks for a roof. (Fairies are not dolls, so dollhouses do not suit them.)

To transform a tree, stump, or rock into a tiny fairy hideaway, make a small door out of almost anything (up to 8 inches tall and 4 to 5 inches wide) and place it at the base. Add an old earring, tack, or other bauble as a door knob. Such an entrance is all that you need to help fairies move easily between our world and theirs.

No back- or front yard? No worries: Make a fairy garden in a container. Use a flowerpot, old wheelbarrow, or window box—even a plastic dishpan. Make sure that it has holes in the bottom for water to drain.

Fill your container with good potting soil. Collect small plants and moss. Put the fairy house into the container on top of the soil mix. Place the accessories around the house. Arrange and rearrange everything until you are happy with the results. Set the plants into the soil and water lightly. Make a path to the front door with pebbles or stones.

Convert to metric on p. 181

THE FIRST FAIRY SELFIES?

In 1917, cousins Frances Griffiths, age 10, and Elsie Wright, age 16, who lived in the English village of Cottingley, borrowed a box camera belonging to Arthur Wright (Elsie's father) and took photos of themselves in the woodlands. When Arthur and Elsie developed the film, they saw fairies in the picture! For decades, many people believed that the photos confirmed the existence of fairies. Not until 1981 did Frances reveal the truth—that she and Elsie had cut the fairies out of paper and fastened them in place with hatpins.

DESIGN, DECORATE, DO-IT-YOURSELF

Collect pinecones, acorn caps, seeds, pebbles, fallen bark, seashells, sticks and twigs, and bits of wood and moss. Ask a parent for some yarn, beads, fabric scraps, or even costume jewelry no longer worn (avoid plastic; fairies are "green"). Use your imagination and these ideas to make natural furniture and accessories:

- Make fairy chairs by using bark for the backing, stones for seats, and twigs for legs, and your fairies will surely linger.
- Make a seesaw from a flat piece of wood balanced on a twig or small stone.
- Turn bent twigs and twine into an arbor.
- Create garden "gazing" balls by gluing marbles to wooden golf tees.
- Tie a tire from a broken toy car or truck to a twig for a fairy-size tire swing.
- Lay flat stones for pathways and a patio or spread sand for a beach.
- Make fences and signposts with craft sticks.
- Use large, upturned seashells as pools, small ones as birdbaths. Fill the shells with blue-color stones (as water) or place a mirror on the ground as a looking-glass pond.
- Arrange or stack pieces of wood or stones as benches and a table. Place acorn-cap bowls at each place setting.
- Put stones in a circle for a campfire and stack twigs as firewood.
- Add one or two fairy statues to show fairies that they are welcome. Sprinkle a bit of fairy dust (glitter), whisper a welcome, and wait for fairies to move in!

MINIATURE PLANTS ARE MAGICAL

Gardens require plants; fairy gardens require small plants to suit fairies' tiny sizes. Many nurseries offer a wide variety of miniature plants that are perfect for fairy gardens. Choose plants with different heights and leaf shapes, small leaves, and colorful, multicolor, or shiny leaves—just as you see in nature. Plants that cover the ground (such as moss) or have small flowers fit in well, as do miniature vines. Water regularly and lightly. If a plant fails, remove it and replace it with another.

THE MOST FAMOUS FAIRY OF ALL . . .

. . . just might be twinkling Tinker Bell, from the play (and book, TV show, and film) *Peter Pan; or The Boy Who Wouldn't Grow Up* by Sir J. M. Barrie. In the story, pirate Captain Hook poisons Tinker Bell, and this makes her light grow dimmer. As he watches her fade away, Peter Pan cries out to the audience or readers, "If you believe [in fairies], clap your hands! Clap! Don't let Tink die!" In every performance and reading, children clap and shout, "I do believe in fairies!" If they are loud enough, Tinker Bell's light grows brighter—a sign that she will live.

PILE ON!

MAKING COMPOST IS EASY, GOOD FOR PLANTS, AND A GREAT WAY TO DISPOSE OF SOME GARBAGE.

Worms and microorganisms eat most of our food waste—eggshells, banana peels, apple cores, and more—and turn it into dark, crumbly stuff called compost.

When compost is mixed into the soil, plants grow better and produce more or bigger flowers, vegetables, and fruit. You can make compost in your own yard. It's easy. Your plants will love you and so will your garbage collectors.

The quickest way to make compost is to find a small place in the corner of your yard that isn't used for anything. (Make sure that the place is okay with your parents.) Now start collecting things that will rot and pile them up there.

1. **Gather some rough "brown" stuff that is high in carbon, such as twigs, corncobs, or crushed nutshells, and place them on your compost spot.**

2. **On top, pile "green" stuff that is high in nitrogen. This would include hair from your hairbrush, grass clippings, dying houseplants or flowers, and kitchen scraps (such as onion skins, fruit cores and peels, lettuce leaves, and coffee grounds).**

3. **Always cover your food scraps. Use grass, leaves, wood chips, soil, or sawdust. This will keep away flies and other pests.**

4. **Next, pile on more browns, such as dried leaves, pine needles, or shredded newspapers.**

5. **Add some garden soil and peat moss on top.**

6. **Soak the pile with water.**

In a week or two, get a garden fork and stir up your pile, turning it over to expose a new surface (in the same place). Soak it again, if it hasn't rained for several days. Every few days, add more greens, burying them deep in the pile. In a week or two, flip the pile back over again. Keep doing that, and in a few months, you'll have compost!

GOOD BROWNS

Corncobs
Dried leaves, shredded
Shredded newspapers
Crushed nutshells
Pine needles
Sawdust
Straw

GOOD GREENS

Coffee grounds
Crushed eggshells
Fruit scraps
Grass clippings
Hair/fur
Tea bag contents
Vegetable scraps

COMPOST KILLERS

Do not add meat, bones, dairy products, fat or grease, or human or pet poop to a compost pile. These ingredients will attract pests (such as raccoons, rats, skunks, bears, and insects) and may pose health hazards.

SWINE'S SNOUT

OTHER WONDERS OF THE PLANT WORLD

Some plants have weird names. They get them in the same way that a pet or food might get its name: from one of their features (think of a dog named Spot) or a person (think of a Baby Ruth candy bar) or the like. Here are a few odd-named wild plants and their tales.

SWINE'S SNOUT

Swine's snout is a wildflower. Its name refers to its flower: After it has matured and is ready to develop seeds, it closes up, forming a shape similar to that of the most prominent part of a pig's face.

Swine's snout is another name for the dandelion—and this name has a story, too. "Dandelion" comes from the French phrase *dent de lion,* meaning "lion's tooth," because the edges of the plant's leaves have a similar shape.

CHEESES

Cheeses, also called cheese weed or cheese mallow, is a sprawling weed. It grows throughout most of North America in yards, gardens, roadsides, and neglected areas. Its name refers to the plant's unusual dry fruit, which resembles a tiny wheel of cheese.

NOSEBLEED

Nosebleed, also called yarrow, is a ferny-leaf plant that grows along roadsides and in neglected fields. Its leaves have been used for centuries to both stop and start a nosebleed. Crushed, rolled-up leaves were placed in the nostrils.

CLASS ACTS

Many plants have one or more common names. To eliminate confusion, scientists developed a method of naming and classifying plants so that each has a unique scientific name.

In the 1750s, biologist Carolus Linnaeus established a two-part naming system. The two parts are called the genus and the species; each word is in Latin. (Linnaeus used Latin because it was a common language among scholars at that time.)

Take the nosebleed plant: It was so useful for healing that legendary Greek warrior Achilles used it to treat the wounds of his soldiers during the Trojan War. The plant now bears the warrior's name as its genus name: *Achillea.* In Latin, *mille* means thousand, and *folium* means leaf. Nosebleed's species name, *millefolium,* refers to the plant's divided, feathery leaves.

Linnaeus also added three higher levels of classification above genus and species. We use a modified version of his system, which includes Kingdom, Phylum, Class, Order, Family, Genus, and Species. These categories enable scientists to organize similar plants together.

To remember the order of plant classification levels, memorize this phrase: King Philip Came Over For Good Spaghetti.

BRITISH SOLDIER LICHEN

This lichen is both a fungus and an alga. The fungus provides a structure upon which the alga can live, and it helps to retain water. The alga provides food for the fungus. You can find ¼-inch-tall British soldier lichen in dry, sunny areas on decaying stumps and logs and in mossy areas. (Toy soldier lichen is similar.)

Convert to metric on p. 181

Look closely, and you'll see tiny red caps at some of the tips of the lichen. (The caps produce fungal spores.) This is probably what led to its name, which refers to the red coats worn by British soldiers during the American Revolutionary War in the 1770s.

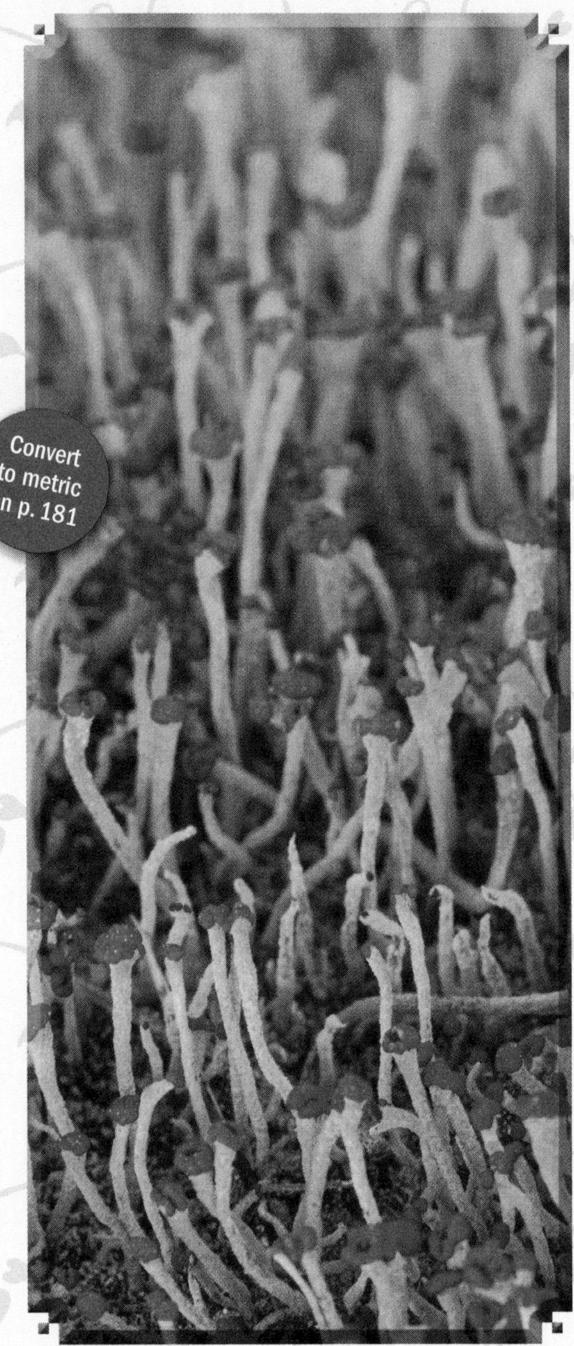

BIRD'S NEST

This wildflower flourishes in the dry soil of fields, roadsides, and neglected areas. It gets its name from its lacy clusters of tiny white flowers that often have one reddish-brown flower in the center. Once insects pollinate the flowers, the entire cluster turns up to form a cup resembling a tiny bird's nest.

Another name for this plant is Queen Anne's lace. This may refer to an 18th-century queen of Britain and Ireland. Legend says that Queen Anne pricked her finger while making lace, drawing a drop of blood (the little red flower). Others claim that the name has connections with a much older St. Anne, who lived in the 1st century B.C. and is the patron saint of lace makers.

The plant is also known as "wild carrot" because its thin roots, when harvested during their first year, can be added to soups and used to flavor teas. The leaves and roots, when crushed, smell like carrots. It is an ancestor of the carrots that we grow in our gardens.

Be careful: Bird's nest has several look-alikes, including poison hemlock, which is—as its name suggests—toxic.

Indigo bunting

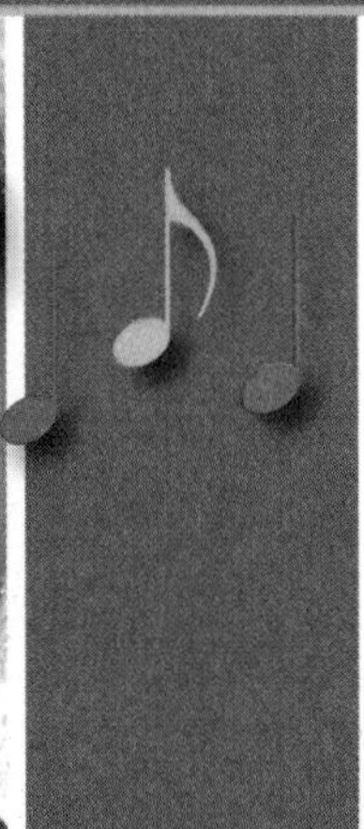

American robin

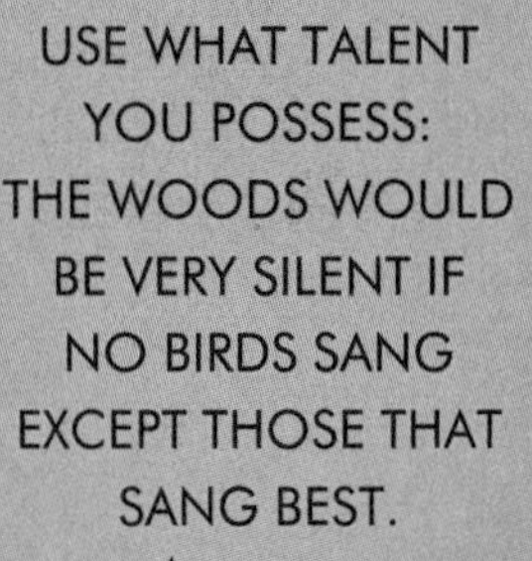

USE WHAT TALENT YOU POSSESS: THE WOODS WOULD BE VERY SILENT IF NO BIRDS SANG EXCEPT THOSE THAT SANG BEST.

–Anonymous

Northern cardinal

Barred owl

Yellow warbler

CALLING ALL BIRDS

Carolina wren

American goldfinches

Humans have been imitating animal sounds for centuries. Roman emperor Julian complained about the sounds in nearby mountains made by hunters who used vocal calls to attract their prey. Yodeling originated with shepherds trying to control their herd while letting their fellow shepherds know their location.

The tradition of producing animal sounds continues today. Here are some kids who have mastered the art.

LOONY TUNES

In 2015, Maret Sotkiewicz and Tyler Ellis teamed up to compete against 14 other students in the annual Piedmont (California) High School bird-calling contest. Created in 1965 by science teacher Leonard J. Waxdeck, the contest was intended to encourage student interest in science and nature and provide an opportunity for students to earn extra credit. Competitors perform a skit that incorporates bird calls and fun facts about the bird they mimic. Students are judged on the authenticity of the call, as well as their poise, delivery, and knowledge about the bird. Today, instead of extra credit, each student receives a chicken trophy.

Maret and Tyler listened to hundreds of bird calls on the Web—high shrills, whistles, and more—before settling on the Pacific loon, in part because the low guttural sound that it makes came naturally to Maret. But this is not to say that it was easy. To more realistically mimic a loon, she had to modify her voice.

The pair planned to perform a two-part mating call known as a "growl duet," with Maret doing the low "growl" and Tyler making the higher-pitch response squawk. Maret covered her mouth with her hands to project more tonal difference and flapped her hands in front of her mouth, while inhaling and compressing her neck and groaning in short bursts. The most difficult part, she says, was timing the different beats for the two parts. They did it, though—and well enough to take first place. Their names were inscribed on the school's competition trophy, and they appeared on the *Late Show with David Letterman.* (The show awarded each of them $200, which qualifies them as professionals and bars them from competing in amateur calling contests.) To anyone thinking of calling, Maret advises, "Have fun with it. Embrace the weirdness and go for it 110 percent."

Pacific loon

WEATHER THAT BIRDS KNOW BEST

- If birds be silent, expect thunder.
- If birds whistle in the early morning in winter, expect frost.
- If a robin sings on the high branch of a tree, it is a sign of fine weather. If one sings near the ground, the weather will be wet.
- When woodpeckers are much heard, rain will follow.

Pyrrhuloxia

ON BEING THE BIRD

Joseph Chan, another Piedmont High School student, entered the 2015 contest with an imitation of the pyrrhuloxia, a bird common to the American Southwest. Growing up, Joseph had listened to his father mimicking the same bird. "I have always known this call," Joseph says, "so I suppose it came fairly easily when it was time to start perfecting it. I just made sure that I was consistent every time I did the call, making sure that my lips were always moist and my throat was cleared." He says that the pyrrhuloxia call is more a whistle than a screech, and he imitated it by puckering his lips together as if to whistle while controlling the tone with his tongue on the roof of his mouth. For this effort, he garnered third place.

Joseph advises novice callers to step into character: "Be the bird! Find a fun bird, or a bird that you can relate to on some level. It makes the learning experience better and makes for a more entertaining call. Just have fun, and don't get discouraged if you can't do it the first time. I couldn't. Just keep at it until you feel like the call has been made your own."

A ROOSTER BOOSTER

Agricultural fairs and expositions throughout the country also host animal-calling contests. At the 2015 Iowa State Fair, Nicholas Stocks from Manchester, Iowa, joined other contestants of ages 7 to 18 who imitated a bevy of barnyard animals—chickens, roosters, ducks, and turkeys. The Iowa contest requires participants to produce a particular animal call using only their own mouth and lungs. Nicholas registered for the Rooster Calling Contest, in what would not be his first appearance; he had entered several years before but gotten nervous and finished only in fourth place. He gained confidence by doing presentations in his 4-H club and has since become more relaxed about performing.

For the 2015 fair, 12-year-old Nicholas practiced only while in the car on the way to the competition. When his turn came, he imitated a rooster's crow by barely touching his tongue to the sides of his mouth and teeth while making a guttural sound—and took home first place. His advice for enthusiasts is simple: "Give it your best shot, and believe in yourself."

Rooster with hen (front)

Tom turkey

Convert to metric on p. 181

YELPER HELPER

Avid outdoorsman Mitch Behilo was inspired to make and use a homemade turkey wing bone call to attract wild turkeys in the woods near his home in Bernardston, Massachusetts. Today, he often leads turkey-spotting field trips for youth with learning disabilities from the school where he works. Mitch teaches the kids how to make different sounds by using their own caller or one that he supplies.

To produce his calls, which are based on a traditional design used by Native Americans, Mitch uses three bones from the wings of turkeys he's harvested. One bone is the bell, which is connected to the shoulder, and the other two are from the wing (and are comparable to the bones in a human forearm). Mitch cuts the bones and cleans out their marrow before gluing the pieces together. (Unlike Native Americans, who used pine pitch to glue the segments together, Mitch uses epoxy.) The finished tool is about 8 inches long and is called a yelper. Mitch hunts only male turkeys (toms), and he uses the yelper to attract them. By placing the narrow end in the corner of his mouth and sucking in, Mitch can produce the yelping call that a female turkey (hen) makes to attract the male bird and signal her location.

Tufted titmice

WORDS OF A FEATHER

CAN YOU FLOCK THEM TOGETHER?
MATCH EACH BIRD WITH ITS CALL.

___ **1.** Indigo bunting
___ **2.** Northern cardinal
___ **3.** Olive-sided flycatcher
___ **4.** American goldfinch
___ **5.** Ovenbird
___ **6.** Barred owl
___ **7.** Great horned owl
___ **8.** California quail
___ **9.** King rail
___ **10.** American robin
___ **11.** White-throated sparrow
___ **12.** Tundra swan
___ **13.** Brown thrasher
___ **14.** Tufted titmouse
___ **15.** Eastern towhee
___ **16.** Red-eyed vireo
___ **17.** Black-throated blue warbler
___ **18.** Chestnut-sided warbler
___ **19.** Yellow warbler
___ **20.** Carolina wren

A. Cheer, cheer, cheer
B. Cheerily, cheer up, cheer up, cheerily, cheer up
C. Chi-CA-go!
D. Drink your tea!
E. Drop it! Drop it! Cover it up! Cover it up! Pull it up! Pull it up!
F. Here I am. Where are you?
G. Hip-hip-hurrah
H. I'm so laz-eee!
I. Old Sam Peabody, Peabody, Peabody
J. Peter, Peter, Peter
K. Pleased, pleased, pleased, pleased ta meetcha
L. Po-ta-to-chip
M. Quick! Three beers!
N. Sweet, sweet, sweet, I am so sweet
O. Tea-cher, Tea-cher, TEA-cher
P. Teakettle, teakettle, teakettle
Q. What? What? Where? Where? See it! See it!
R. Who cooks for you? Who cooks for you all?
S. Who's awake? Me, too!
T. Woo-hoo

ANSWERS 1. Q; **2.** A; **3.** M; **4.** L; **5.** O; **6.** R; **7.** S; **8.** C; **9.** G; **10.** B; **11.** I; **12.** T; **13.** E; **14.** J; **15.** D; **16.** F; **17.** H; **18.** K; **19.** N; **20.** P

FOOD FOR THE BIRD FEEDER

	SUNFLOWER SEEDS	MILLET	THISTLE SEEDS	SAFFLOWER SEEDS	CRACKED CORN	PEANUTS	PEANUT BUTTER	SUET	RAISINS	APPLES	ORANGES AND GRAPEFRUIT
Cardinal	•	•		•	•				•	•	•
Chickadee	•	•		•	•	•	•	•			
Finch	•	•	•	•	•	•	•				•
Goldfinch	•		•								
Junco	•	•	•	•	•						
Nuthatch	•	•		•		•	•	•			
Sparrow	•	•		•	•	•					
Titmouse	•	•		•	•	•	•	•			
Woodpecker						•	•	•			

WELCOME TO OUR MOOSE-EUM!

The moose first came to North America from Siberia 10,000 to 14,000 years ago. Since then, it has made its home across the northern half of the continent, mostly inhabiting forested areas with moist conditions. Moose feed on plants, which is surprising to many, considering their giant size and staggering strength. In fact, moose are known for being so strong and fast that some countries used to attempt to train them to be ridden in combat in place of horses. Unfortunately for those trainers, moose are also smart, and they would hide at the first sign of any real danger.

Moose Lingo

BULL: male moose
CALF: baby moose
COW: female moose
SHEDS: antlers that have dropped off, or been shed, after the mating period. Some people collect them—an illegal act in national parks and other protected areas.
YARD: thickly wooded area where, in the winter, moose gather for mutual protection and to trample the snow for easier access to food.

Moose on the Hoof

Moose are large, heavy animals that are most commonly found in areas with soft ground. This means that they need big feet to help them distribute their weight so that they will not sink. Moose tracks are big, and the shape of the track is long, narrow, and almost like a heart, with the point of the heart facing the direction the moose is traveling. Each track is split down the middle into two parts. These are the moose's two big toes. The moose also has two other smaller toes, but they are raised and therefore do not register in the track.

So Nice They Named It Twice

The moose is one of the few animals whose scientific genus and species names are the same words.

- American bison: *Bison bison*
- Badger: *Meles meles*
- Black rat: *Ratus ratus*
- Gorilla: *Gorilla gorilla*
- Green iguana: *Iguana iguana*
- Moose: *Alces alces*
- Sally Lightfoot red crab: *Grapsus grapsus*

A Moos-age for Moose Lovers

Seeing a moose in real life is exciting and a lot of fun. However, when tracking moose or moose-watching, always be aware that moose can sometimes become aggressive and charge. Because of their immense size and speed, this can be a very dangerous situation. To avoid it, always keep your distance when observing a moose and be careful never to come between a cow and her calf.

Where Moose Are on the Loose

1. Glacier Bay National Park, Alaska: This marine wilderness park is accessible only by plane or boat. Visitors are greeted by not only moose, but also caribou, grizzly bears, and Dall sheep.

2. Isle Royale National Park, Michigan: In the early 1900s, many moose swam to this 45-mile-long island in Lake Superior and took up residence. Their offspring live here now.

3. Moosehead Lake, Maine: The largest lake in its region, Moosehead Lake can offer fantastic views of moose from its hiking trails, from along Route 15, or from a canoe on the lake.

4. Algonquin Provincial Park, Ontario: Some believe this to be the best moose watching site in North America. One visitor claimed to have seen 10 moose in one day here. A great time to visit is during late spring, when moose are often on the roads, drinking the salty runoff.

Q: What has antlers and sucks your blood?

A: A moose-quito

Five Signs a Moose Doesn't Like You . . . and What to Do About It

Moose are easily frightened. Whether you're in a car, hiking, or hunting, if you look threatening to a bull or come between a cow and her calf, you could be charged. Here are signs that a moose feels it is in danger:

1. The moose is heading toward you.
2. It is grunting and stomping.
3. It is throwing its head around.
4. It has its ears pointed back.
5. The hairs on its back are raised.

If you see this, the best thing to do is to keep your eyes on the moose, hold up your hands with palms out, speak softly, and put something solid—tree, boulder, vehicle—between you and the charging moose as quickly as possible. Some people say that if you run, a moose will not chase you for long before giving up (but moose are very fast!). If a moose knocks you down, curl up, play dead, and protect your head.

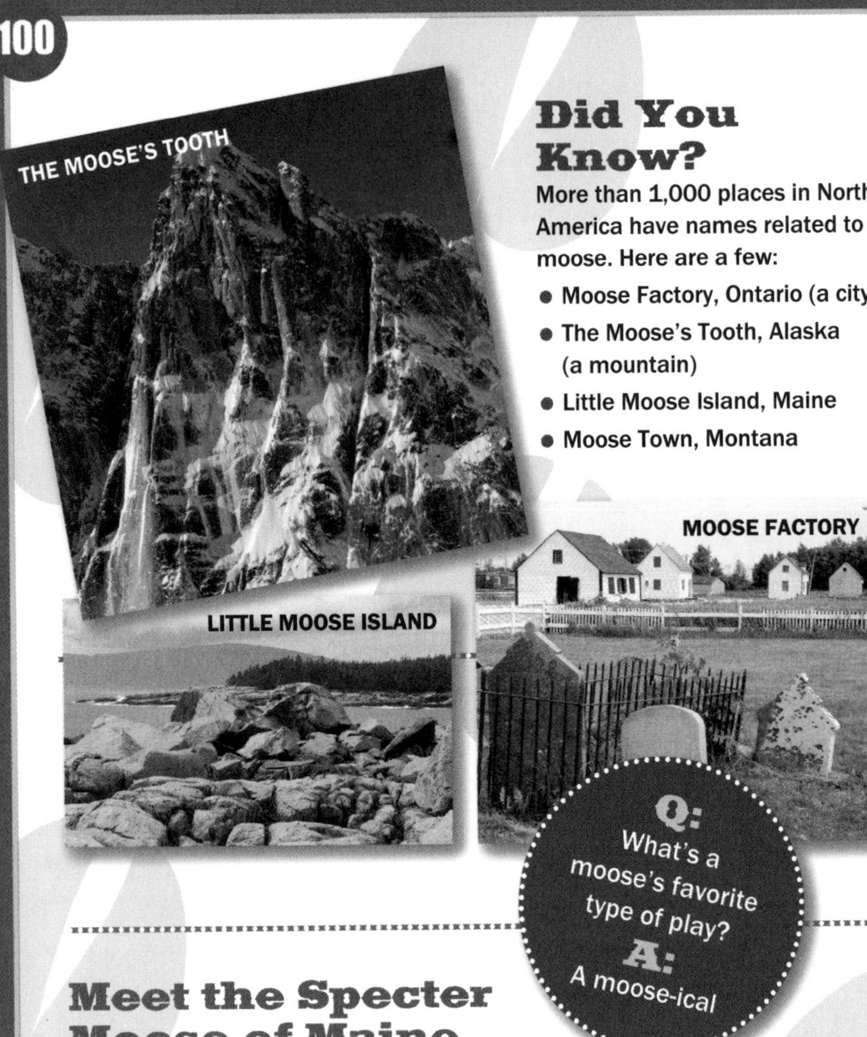

Did You Know?

More than 1,000 places in North America have names related to moose. Here are a few:

- Moose Factory, Ontario (a city)
- The Moose's Tooth, Alaska (a mountain)
- Little Moose Island, Maine
- Moose Town, Montana

Q: What's a moose's favorite type of play?

A: A moose-ical

Meet the Specter Moose of Maine

Popular folklore tells of a giant white moose that wanders the woods of Maine. All who have seen it report that it stands around 13 feet tall, with an antler span of 10 feet. Its weight has been estimated at no less than 2,500 pounds. (Compare this to the largest moose taken in Maine to date, which had a dressed weight of 1,330 pounds, meaning that its total weight was probably around 1,767 pounds.) The Maine monster moose was first spotted in 1891 by a hunting guide and was seen several more times during the early 20th century. During this time, there were reports that it was immune to bullets and chased hunters. However, legend has it that it carried a man and woman back to safety after they had become stranded in the woods.

Momentous Moose Matters

- In Europe, moose are called elk.
- Moose can sustain a running speed of almost 22 miles per hour and can go even faster in short bursts.
- Moose are able to swim as far as 7½ miles and can dive as far down as 18 feet to reach succulent plants.

Convert to metric on p. 181

- Moose are the largest members of the deer family. The Alaskan subspecies can grow to be more than 8 feet tall and top 1,800 pounds. The more southern its habitat, the smaller the moose, in general.
- Traditional lore from several European countries states that medicine from a moose's hind foot can cure epilepsy.

The name "moose" originates from the Algonquian names mus and moos, meaning "eater of twigs" and "he who strips bark."

AN UNLIKELY FRIENDSHIP

In 1999, a crow appeared in the yard of Ann and Wally Collito in North Attleboro, Massachusetts. The couple watched in amazement as it befriended a stray black-and-white kitten. (Cats and crows are usually enemies!) The crow, acting like the kitten's mother, fed it bugs and worms. For a while, Ann said, the kitten trusted only the bird. Eventually, the kitten trusted the couple, so they adopted her and named her Cassie. They called the crow Moses. Every morning at 6:00, Moses pecked on their screen door to summon Cassie. Cassie and Moses played together for 5 years before Moses disappeared.

LOVE BY THE BEAKFUL

As a preschooler, Gabi Mann of Seattle, Washington, sometimes dropped morsels of food in her yard by accident. A few crows noticed, swooped down, and devoured the treats. Soon, the crows began watching for Gabi. When she and her brother headed to the school bus stop, they scattered tidbits from their lunch bags. The crows gobbled those scraps, too, and returned to the bus stop in the afternoon, hoping for more. By 2013, Gabi and her mother were putting out fresh water, peanuts, and dry dog food for the crows each morning. That's when Gabi started getting gifts from the crows in return: small, shiny things that the birds could carry in their beaks, such as pieces of sea glass, buttons, paper clips, beads, and earrings. By 2015, when Gabi turned 8, she had a collection of trinkets, each labeled with a story about where and when the crows had left it. Her most prized gift is a small, pearl-color heart, which she says shows how much the crows love her.

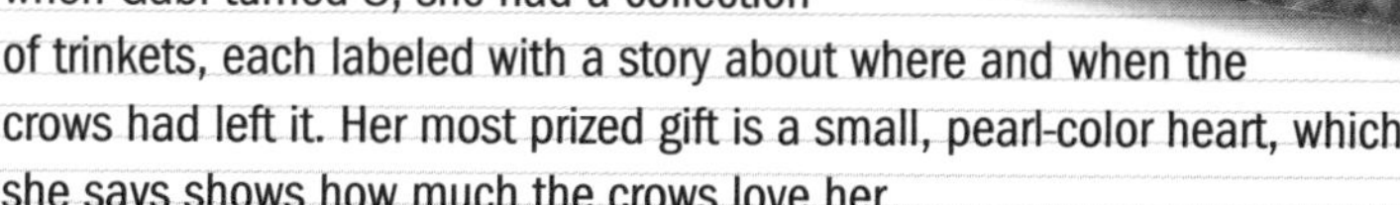

Good, Bad, and Lucky Crows

- Crows are helpful: They eat garbage, dead animals, and insects that damage crops.
- Crows can harm crops. Since ancient times, farmers have been using "scarecrows" (get it?) to frighten birds away from their plants.
- In some cultures, including Native American, crows are seen as bringing good luck. In some myths, fables, and legends, crows are presented as tricksters, liars, and thieves.

GET TO KNOW THE CROW

Found in many parts of the world, crows are large black birds with a reputation for being loud and clever. Scientifically speaking, they belong to the genus *Corvus,* which includes crows, ravens, and rooks. They are also part of the Corvidae family, along with jays, magpies, and nutcrackers—some of the smartest of all birds. A common type, the American crow, is found over much of the United States year-round and in many parts of Canada during the summer.

You might recognize a crow's "caw, caw" call. Crows are chatty birds, with more than 20 calls, and "conversations" that can be several minutes long.

Crows eat almost anything, from earthworms and baby birds to roadkill and garbage. They do not usually bother with bird feeders. Look for crows in open areas near woods, parks, dumps, campgrounds, athletic fields, and parking lots. To attract them, put out unsalted peanuts, dry pet food, and even french fries on the ground in areas with both trees and open space. If you regularly feed them, you might find them waiting for you another day. They may even follow you!

CROWS LOVE A CROWD (OF OTHER CROWS!)

These social birds often sleep together in large groups, called roosts, especially in fall and winter. Roosts may contain fewer than a hundred birds or many, many more. A famous roost in Fort Cobb, Oklahoma, was estimated to include more than 2 million crows!

Watch out: Crows have been known to dive-bomb people if they get too close to nests containing their young babies, or fledglings.

Scientists have several theories about why crows enjoy big slumber parties. The birds may be trying to get to the safest, most comfortable spot, and they probably feel more protected from enemies when in large groups. They could also be spying to see where other crows fly to find food.

Crows like urban areas because they are often warmer, have fewer owl enemies, and provide lights to help them watch for enemies. But large roosts in cities can turn into a noisy mess for people, leaving parks and sidewalks covered with bird droppings.

Light and sound can scare the birds without hurting them. After about 20,000 crows started hanging out in Albany, New York, a group from the U.S. Department of Agriculture Wildlife Services used flares, bullhorns, and nonharmful lasers to chase them away. Similar methods have been used in Pennsylvania, New Jersey, and Connecticut.

CROWS KNOW

Crows can hold grudges. Researchers in Seattle, Washington, did scans of crows' brains and determined that their brains "light up" when they see the threatening face of someone they have seen before.

In a separate study, birds were captured by researchers who wore one type of "threatening" mask, and the birds were then fed by researchers wearing a different type of "caring" mask. The crows could tell the difference.

Talking Crow

"A murder of crows" is a flock of crows.

"As the crow flies" refers to distance measured in a straight line.

"Crow's-feet" are wrinkles at the corners of a person's eyes.

"To be up with the crows" means to be awake early in the morning.

"To crow" about something means to brag or boast.

"To eat crow" means to admit that you are wrong.

BIRD BRAINS

A crow's brain is about the size of a human thumb, and crows are about as smart as a typical 7-year-old human. Get this:

- Aesop's fables, a collection written more than 2,000 years ago, include the story of a crow whose beak did not reach the water in a half-full pitcher. The bird drops pebbles into the pitcher until the water level rises enough for it to get a drink.

  In an experiment, modern scientists put a half-full pitcher of water in the presence of several crows. Like the one in the fable, these crows wisely dropped rocks into the water to raise the water level.

- In Japan, observers watched crows carefully place walnuts on crosswalks in front of cars that had stopped for a red light. The crows waited for the stoplight to change to green and then picked up the nut meats after the cars had run over and cracked open the nuts.

- The New Caledonian crow has been called the smartest of all crows. It uses its beak to make tools out of twigs and leaves to catch bugs that it finds in hard-to-reach places.

Getting Antsy

Sometimes crows and other birds sit on anthills and let ants crawl all over their bodies. Some birds chomp on the ants and rub themselves in their remains. Scientists call this "anting" and are not sure why it occurs. They suggest that ants produce formic acid that may act as an insect repellent or an oily liquid that may help to soothe the birds' skin as they lose their feathers.

TINY HEROES Among Us

They're everywhere—not just at your picnic!

Ants have been around since the days of the dinosaurs, and they inhabit just about every corner of Earth. They are one of the most successful of insects, with more than 11,000 species, outnumbering all other individual animals combined.

Ants, or emmets, live in colonies made up almost entirely of nonmating female workers whose job it is to gather food, build the nest, and look after the egg-laying queen and her young. At certain times, winged males and females are produced by the queen for the purpose of mating with ants from other colonies. After mating, the male ants die and the mated queens fly off, shed their wings, and start new colonies.

Although some species, such as the carpenter ant and the stinging fire ant, are considered pests, in general ants are thought of as beneficial. Most ants nest in the ground, digging a maze of tunnels that allow air and moisture to get to the roots of plants. The leaves and dead insects brought into the nest decay and fertilize the plants above. Many ants are predators and feed on insects that attack lawns and gardens. In the process of gathering food, they sometimes pollinate certain plants and distribute seeds.

A sudden convergence of ants in the garden or a line of ants moving up and down a tree usually indicates the presence of aphids, mealybugs, or other sap-sucking insects that attack plants. These insects produce a substance called "honeydew" (not to be confused with the sweet green melon with the pale green rind). The ants stroke the insects with their antennas, causing the insects to excrete the sweet liquid. The ants swallow it and store it in a special holding stomach called the crop. The honeydew is brought back to the nest and shared with the queen and other workers. Some ants even keep aphids in their nest as a farmer would keep a cow, giving them food and shelter in exchange for honeydew.

TINY TASTES

In some cultures, ants are delicacies. The honey-pot ants that live in the deserts of the U.S. Southwest gather large amounts of nectar and store it in the swollen bodies of specialized worker ants called repletes. Native Americans have snacked on these sweet ants for centuries.

WEATHER ANT-ICS

- Expect stormy weather when ants travel in a straight line; when they scatter all over, the weather will be fine.
- An open ant hole indicates clear weather; a closed one, an approaching storm.
- If ant hills are high in July, the coming winter will be hard.

Q: What is the biggest ant in the world?

A: A gi-ant!

SNORE LORE

Dreaming of ants foretells health and wealth.

THE ANT, OR EMMET

These emmets, how little they are in our eyes!
We tread them to dust, and a troop of them dies,
  Without our regard or concern;
Yet, as wise as we are, if we went to their school,
There's many a sluggard, and many a fool,
  Some lessons of wisdom might learn.

They don't wear their time out in sleeping or play,
But gather up corn in a sunshiny day,
  And for winter they lay up their stores.
They manage their work in such regular forms
One would think they foresaw all the frosts and the storms,
  And so brought their food within doors.

–Isaac Watts, hymn writer (1674–1748)

LEAVE IT TO THE BEAVER

ALTHOUGH SOMETIMES CALLED THE "AMERICAN BEAVER," *CASTOR CANADENSIS* IS BELOVED BY CANADA, TOO. HOW MUCH DO YOU KNOW ABOUT THIS BIG-TAILED BUDDY?

Convert to metric on p. 181

A BEAVER MEASURES, ON AVERAGE, 45 INCHES FROM NOSE TIP TO THE BLUNT END OF ITS FOOTLONG TAIL.

The beaver is the biggest rodent in North America and the second largest in the Americas. (South America's capybara is the largest.)

Beavers waddle awkwardly on land but use their powerful webbed back feet to swim with ease. They can reach speeds of up to 5 miles per hour!

A BEAVER'S FRONT TEETH ARE COATED WITH HARD ORANGE ENAMEL, AND THEY NEVER STOP GROWING.

Beavers' front teeth are continually sharpened against each other as the beaver gnaws at trees and branches. They have lips that close behind their incisors, which allows them to gnaw underwater.

ON COLD WINTER DAYS, YOU CAN TELL IF A BEAVER LODGE IS "OCCUPIED" BY THE "STEAM" FROM THEIR BREATH RISING THROUGH THE VENT AT THE TOP.

Cameras inside beaver dens have revealed that muskrats, mice, moths, and voles sometimes hang out in the lodge.

BEAVERS DO MUCH OF THEIR WORK AT NIGHT.

Beavers construct dams and lodges from sticks and mud, inspect them daily, and make regular repairs—and renovations. The beaver is one of the few mammals that will change a not-quite-perfect place to suit its needs.

Beavers build canals to move building materials and link ponds together for travel. In autumn, they embed some tender timber underwater as a food cache; in winter, they retrieve it from below the ice.

TRUE OR FALSE?

(Answers below.)

1. Beavers eat fish.

2. Beavers plan which way the trees they cut will fall.

3. Beavers as big as black bears once built lodges across North America.

4. Beavers are often killed by trees they fell.

Convert to metric on p. 181

1. False. They're vegetarian.

2. Scientists disagree. Some studies suggest that this is true; others, that it's not. More study is needed.

3. True. About 10,000 years ago, they were gnawing down trees with their 6-inch incisors.

4. False. The major threats to them are predators, disease, starvation, and the enduring one: human activity.

CANADA'S BEAVER FEVER

- In Canada's largest national park, Wood Buffalo, which spans Alberta and the Northwest Territories, beavers have made a dam that can be seen from outer space. It stretches 2,789 feet and might be the world's longest.

- Canada's first postage stamp—the "3-penny beaver"—was also the first in the world to picture an animal. Issued in April 1851, it was designed by Sir Sandford Fleming. This rare stamp is valued at around $120,000.
- The first steamship on Canada's west coast arrived in Vancouver in 1836. Its name? *Beaver.*
- The beaver became Canada's official emblem in 1975.
- Canada's 5-cent piece has featured a beaver since 1968 (and during three other multiyear periods before that).

MOON LORE

November's full Moon was called the **Beaver Moon** by both the colonists and the Algonquin tribes because this was the time to set beaver traps before the swamps froze, to ensure a supply of warm winter furs.

Other tribes gave the Moon other names, based on their observations:

- Full Frost Moon
- Moon When the Rivers Begin to Freeze
- Snowy Mountains in the Morning Moon
- Geese Going Moon

AUTUMN BEAVER

Hurry, Beaver, build your home.
Shape it in a stately dome.
Autumn Beaver, here's a scheme:
Fell a tree and block the stream.
Make a pond that's wide and deep.
Build a den in which to sleep.
On the shoreline, cut a limb.
With your webbed feet, push and swim.
Gnaw some branches. Gather sticks.
Put some mud into the mix.
Bark and leaves will cover walls.
You'll be busy as night falls.
Store up herbs and grasses sweet.
Save them for a winter's treat.
Slap your tail to give alarm.
Keep your family safe from harm.
Fill your lodge with kits and mate.
Hurry, Beaver, don't be late.

–Stephanie Shaw

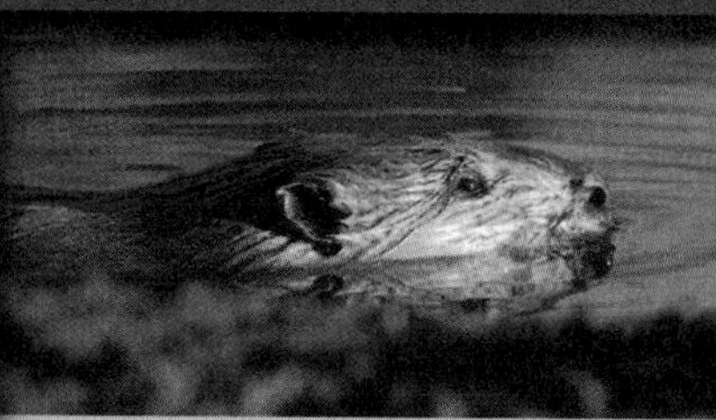

OTHER BEAVER BITS

Oregon is called the Beaver State (unofficially) because in the early 19th century, its rivers and streams were a source of beaver pelts for trappers *(18 hats could be made from one pelt!)*. The trappers' routes became known as the Oregon Trail, the path taken by thousands of pioneers in the 1840s.

A Few Bars

You use soap every day! What's the story behind this sudsy stuff?

Soap comes in bars, powders, and liquids—it's even on a rope! No matter its shape, size, scent, or color, soap is made from a mixture of sodium or potassium salts and natural oils and fats. Soap works because a chemical process breaks down grease and dirt every time that you use it with water.

THE EXACT ORIGINS of soap are a bit like dirty water: murky. Believe it or not, at first soap was used as medicine to treat skin diseases. One problem with early soap was that it was made from animal fat and lye. Lye is made with ashes, and it can burn skin and even cause blindness. Use of impure beef fat could make the early soap stinky, too.

EARLY GREEKS cleaned themselves with stuff like clay, sand, and ashes—not soap. Sumerians were mixing fat, ashes, and water by 3,000 B.C. Their ancient tablets contain soap-making directions. The Celts made a concoction that they called *saipo*.

ANCIENT ROMANS used soap but not in the famous Roman baths. Instead, bathers might rub their body with oil or have someone scrape off their sweat and dirt with a tool that looked like a small rake.

About Soap

ROMAN LEGEND says that the word "soap" comes from a mythical place called Mount Sapo, where animals were sacrificed to the gods. There, rainwater mixed ashes with the fat from these animals and flowed into the Tiber River. According to legend, people at the river discovered that this sudsy mixture could be useful for washing clothes.

BY THE MIDDLE AGES, soap-making had become a trade, or skill. Recipes were secretly passed from generation to generation. Yet, because soap was heavily taxed, only the rich could afford it. People who didn't have access to soap were pretty grungy. So were their clothes. Many folks wore perfume so that they wouldn't smell other people!

IN THE 1600S, chemists began to study the soap-making process. Milder soaps were developed that could be used on fine cloth and lace without ruining them. Several soap makers were among the colonists who came ashore in Jamestown, Virginia, in 1608.

DURING THE 18th- and 19th-century Industrial Revolution, soap factories were built, and as running water and bathtubs became more common, more people were using soap. By 1850, soap-making was one of America's fastest-growing industries.

Detergent, the Pseudo Soap

During World War I, the fats needed for making soap were in short supply. In 1916, the first "detergent" was developed from chemicals and a variety of raw materials in Germany. This manufactured cleaning agent contains no animal fat (this means that detergents are not true soap). After World War II, this industry exploded, as companies developed all sorts of new laundry and dishwashing detergents.

Convert to metric on p. 181

Amazingly Clean World Records

- Gary Pearlman created the largest free-floating soap bubble by using two fishing poles with string tied between them in Cleveland, Ohio, on June 20, 2015. Its volume was 3,399.7 cubic feet.
- In 2009, Carol Vaughn of Britain established a world record with her collection of more than 1,300 different bars of soap from around the world.
- The world's largest bar of soap weighed 15.9 tons. A soap company in Shandong, China, made it in 2015.
- Somehow, 214 people managed to stand inside a very large soap bubble in Prague, Czech Republic, on March 1, 2014.

Handy Help

Clean hands help you to avoid illness and spreading germs. Always wash your hands . . .

- before eating and cooking
- after using the bathroom, blowing your nose, or sneezing
- after handling raw meat
- after touching garbage
- before and after your hands are near your face
- after touching animals or cleaning up after them

HERE'S HOW:

Scrub your hands with warm water and soap for 20 seconds. That's as long as it takes to hum two choruses of the "Happy Birthday" song or this little ditty (sung to the tune of "If You're Happy and You Know It"):

Oh, I wish I was a little bar of soap, bar of soap
Oh, I wish I was a little bar of soap, bar of soap
I'd go slidey, slidey, slidey over every-body's hidey
Oh, I wish I was a little bar of soap, bar of soap.

SOAPY SHOWS

"Soap operas" are not musicals about soap. They are daytime television and radio programs that are known for being very dramatic. The shows earned this nickname because in the 1930s the first advertisers were often soap makers.

Keep the Environment Clean, Too

Some soaps today contain antibacterial agents, ingredients added to kill germs. Many scientists say that these agents are not needed and that their widespread use is harming the environment. Scientists also fear that germs can become stronger as they grow resistant to these agents. Many advise against using antibacterial soap. There are plenty of other ways to come clean!

Get Creative: Carve a Bar!

Soap-carving has been a fun camp and Scout activity for years. It's a traditional art form in Thailand, where artists often carve elaborate flowers and then paint their masterpieces in bright colors. Try your hand at it!

YOU WILL NEED:

- newspaper or old towel to cover the work area
- plastic knives or kitchen butter knives
- sandpaper
- a bar of soap (Ivory works well)
- blank or graph paper for making a pattern (optional)
- pencil
- scissors
- toothpicks, fork, vegetable peeler

1. Cover your work area with newspaper. If using plastic knives, rub sandpaper on the serrated edges to eliminate them. If you like, leave the serration on one knife to use to give your soap texture.

(You can skip steps 2 and 3 by using a marker to outline your shape directly on the bar of soap, if you feel especially confident.)

2. Trace your soap bar on the paper. Within the tracing, draw an outline of the shape that you want to carve, such as a fish, turtle, heart, polar bear, bird, or your initials—use your imagination. Using scissors, cut out the shape.

3. Trace the shape onto your soap bar.

4. Using the knife, begin carving, removing small bits of soap at a time. (If you try to remove too much at once, you might break the soap bar.)

5. As the shape emerges, use the other tools to add details.

6. Gather the soap scraps from your carving, dampen them with a little water, and wad them into a ball. Use to wash hands.

Make a Soap Bar

Molds, glycerin soap, and dyes are available at craft stores.

YOU WILL NEED:

cooking spray, olive oil, or petroleum jelly
heat-resistant mold or plastic cup
1 block glycerin soap
microwave-safe bowl
craft dye (not food coloring)
wooden craft stick or chopstick
objects such as small plastic toys, marbles, coins, or rope that fit(s) in the cup or mold

1. Coat the mold lightly with spray, oil, or petroleum jelly.

2. Break the glycerin into pieces. Put a few pieces into the bowl and microwave on high for 10 to 15 seconds at a time until melted. (The liquid soap is hot. Ask an adult for help.)

3. Put 1 to 2 drops of dye into the liquid soap and stir with a stick.

4. Pour the liquid soap into the mold to cover the bottom of the container or fill halfway, depending on the size of the object(s). Let cool for about 20 minutes. Place the object(s) on top of the hardened layer of soap. If using rope, put both ends into the mold (leaving a loop of rope out of it).

6. Add the remaining liquid soap to cover. Set it aside for 2 hours to cool and harden. Carefully remove the soap from the mold.

BIG HELPS FOR LITTLE HURTS

The next time you need some help with your health, check the pantry for these old-fashioned remedies.

SMILING THROUGH CHAPPED OR CRACKED LIPS?

Before you go to bed, coat your lips with honey, which can help to prevent infection as well as to moisturize cracked lips. Or dab some coconut oil on the dry area. Coconut oil is loaded with moisturizing minerals.

ALLERGIES LEAVING YOU STUFFED UP?

Drink hot or iced peppermint tea. The menthol in peppermint helps to thin mucus.

TOO MUCH POOL TIME CAUSING SWIMMER'S EAR?

Carefully place a few drops of white vinegar inside the aching ear. Vinegar has antibacterial and antifungal properties.

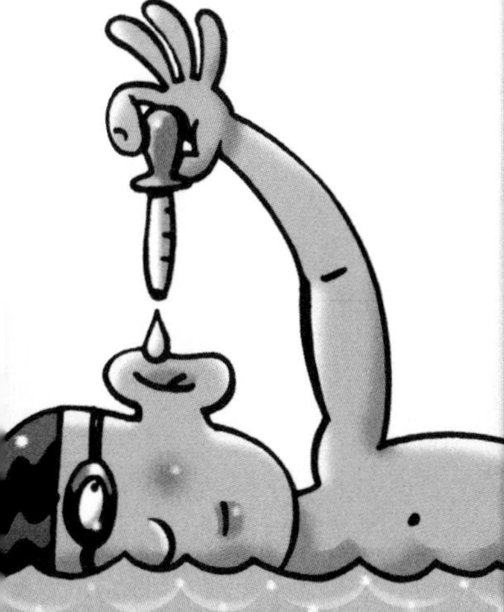

STUNG BY A BEE?

Remove the stinger, then cover the area with lots of toothpaste. Its alkalinity helps to neutralize the acidic venom. (If swelling develops on other body parts, see a doctor immediately.)

INSECT BITES BUGGING YOU?

Cover the bite with a slice of onion for at least 30 minutes. Onions contain sulfur, which breaks down the venom and leaches out the toxin, and flavonoids that encourage healing.

PLAGUED BY PESKY POISON IVY?

Relieve the itch with a pantry paste: Mix together 3 teaspoons of baking soda with 1 teaspoon of water. Apply to the rash. Allow the paste to dry completely. Repeat as necessary. The baking soda will dry out the area.

WARM WEATHER CAUSING EMBARRASSING BODY ODOR?

It's normal and easy to overcome. Dust areas of excessive sweating with cornstarch daily. Cornstarch absorbs moisture.

BURN YOURSELF ON THE GRILL OR STOVETOP?

Soak the burn in cool water for 5 minutes. Soften cabbage leaves in a bowl of hot water, then tear into small pieces. Place the leaves on the burn, cover with gauze, and apply pressure. Cabbage is loaded with glutamine, which aids new cell growth and provides protection against infection.

INDIGESTION AFTER EATING TOO MUCH?

Have a slice of papaya or kiwi. Both of these fruit can help to ease stomach discomfort. (Some people may be allergic to these fruit.)

GOT A TOOTHACHE FROM TOO MUCH CANDY?

Position two cloves (a spice with a pointed end) in your mouth between the aching tooth and your cheek so that the cloves stay in place. Cloves contain eugenol, which is both an anesthetic and an antiseptic.

FEELING DROWSY IN THE AFTERNOON AS THE DAYS GROW SHORTER?

Eat apricots, apples, grapes, pears, and oranges to stay alert. These fruit boost serotonin levels that increase your energy. (And get to bed early!)

TALES OF TIME KEEPERS

FOR NEARLY 200,000 YEARS, PEOPLE LIVED WITHOUT CLOCKS. THEY USED THE POSITION OF THE SUN TO MEASURE THE PASSAGE OF DAYLIGHT HOURS. THEN, THEY FOUND BETTER WAYS TO KEEP TIME.

3500 B.C.
Egyptians build the Sun clock, a four-sided stone pillar, or obelisk. On sunny days, the direction of its shadow indicates morning or afternoon.

SAMPLE SUN CLOCK

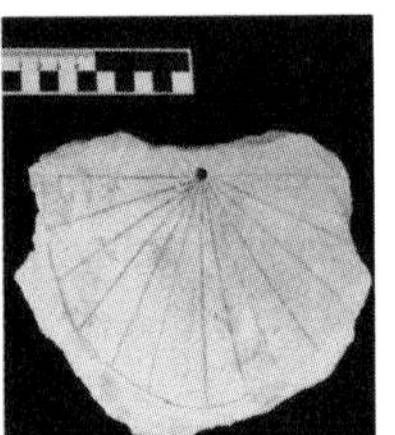

EARLY SUNDIAL

1500 B.C.
Egyptians invent sundials. An upright piece (gnomon) casts a shadow on a flat surface marked with lines to indicate periods of time. As the Sun moves, so does the shadow—but only in daylight.

To measure time at night and on cloudy days, Egyptians begin using water clocks—stone bowls with a small hole in the bottom through which water drips. The bowl's water level indicates the time.

EARLY WATER CLOCK

600 B.C.
The Egyptians create the merkhet, a horizontal bar with a plumb line (a string with a weight on the end) attached to a wooden handle. Using two of these instruments, a person can align certain stars to estimate the time of night.

1ST CENTURY A.D.
The hourglass is

HOURGLASS

first used by the Greeks and Romans.

9TH CENTURY
Candle clocks come into use: When one burns out, a set amount of time has elapsed, usually 4 hours. If a nail is pressed into a candle at a specific (hour) mark and the candle burns

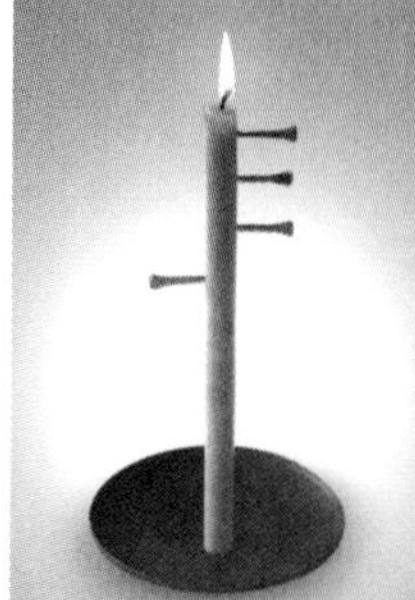
EARLY CANDLE CLOCK

to this mark, the nail falls out onto a metal tray, making a "clink"—the first alarm clock.

1088
In China, Buddhist monk Su Song builds a nearly 40-foot-high tower clock that shows the position of stars,

phases of the Moon, time of day, and day of the month. It is powered by a water wheel: Every 15 minutes, the weight of the water triggers doors opening and figures coming out to strike bells.

EARLY TO MID–14TH CENTURY
Mechanical escapement handless clocks appear in Italian monastery towers. A weight falls, or "escapes," at regular intervals, causing the gears

TOWER ESCAPEMENT

to move. An alarm alerts the keeper, who rings a bell.

14TH CENTURY
The first known mechanical alarm clock is the German iron wall clock with a bell. Until now, most people depended on a crowing rooster to wake them.

1500–1570
Locksmith Peter Henlein of Nuremberg,

NUREMBERG EGG

Germany, invents the mainspring for spring-driven clocks. Called Nuremberg eggs, these small clocks have only an hour hand. They are portable but, being made of iron, are also heavy.

Convert to metric on p. 181

JOST BURGI CLOCK

1577

An astronomer needs an accurate clock for stargazing, so Swiss clockmaker Jost Burgi invents the minute hand.

17TH CENTURY

For years, a small watch on a ribbon worn around the neck was called a pendant watch. When men lost interest in this style, pocket watches came into being. French inventor Blaise Pascal ties his pocket watch to his wrist with a piece of string.

PENDANT WATCH

PENDULUM CLOCK

1656

Dutch scientist Christiaan Huygens makes the pendulum clock. This weight-driven escapement clock's accuracy is within 1 minute per day, but later improves to 10 seconds per day. About this time, use of the minute hand becomes popular. In 1676, Huygens develops the balance wheel and spring assembly still used in some wristwatches.

LATE 1600s

The first "long case," or grandfather, clock is made in England. With its weight-driven escapement and adjustable pendulum weight, it is quite accurate. The name "grandfather clock" originated with Henry Clay Work in 1876. He learned of a long case clock in a hotel owned by two brothers. On the day that one brother died, the clock began losing time. Later, when the other brother died, the clock stopped. This incident inspires Work's song titled "My Grandfather's Clock."

GRANDFATHER CLOCK

18TH CENTURY

Lamp clocks measure time and provide light. Oil drains from a glass container,

THE STUDY AND ART OF MEASURING TIME OR MAKING CLOCKS IS CALLED HOROLOGY, FROM THE GREEK WORD *HÓRA* FOR HOUR AND THE SUFFIX "-OLOGY," MEANING "STUDY OF."

THE WORD "CLOCK" COMES FROM THE MEDIEVAL LATIN *CLOCCA*, MEANING BELL.

EARLY LAMP CLOCK

with time periods marked on it, into a tube with a candlewick. As the oil burns, one can see how much time has elapsed.

1761
John Harrison of England invents the first sea clock, or chronometer. Highly accurate, it helps seamen to determine time zones, or longitude, and decipher their exact positions, preventing many navigational errors and deaths. The chronometer is still used aboard ships.

1787
Levi Hutchins of Concord, New Hampshire, invents a mechanical alarm clock that rings only at 4:00 A.M. because that is when he wants to wake up.

1807
In Connecticut, Eli Terry operates a factory that produces clocks. Until now, all clocks have been handmade.

WRISTWATCH

1810
French watchmaker Abraham Breguet makes the first true wristwatch.

1815
The first battery-powered electric clock is invented by Francis Ronalds. Its large battery sits beside the clock in a concrete box.

1816
Louis Moinet invents the chronograph, with two second hands: one for the time of day, the other to measure specific time periods, as in sporting events. More than one competitor can be timed with it.

CHRONOGRAPH

STOPWATCH

1869
The stopwatch, mass-produced by TAG Heuer Co. of Switzerland, can be stopped and reset to zero. Racers can be timed to hundredths of a second.

1876
A mechanical windup alarm

EARLY ALARM CLOCK

clock that can be set for any time is manufactured by Seth Thomas Company of Connecticut.

1906
The self-contained battery-driven clock eliminates winding.

1914–1918
Soldiers are given wristwatches to replace pendant or pocket watches

SOLDIER'S WRISTWATCH

that require the use of two hands to check—a risk in combat.

1918
Small electric motors replace batteries in clocks.

1923
The self-winding wristwatch is patented by John Harwood in England. It winds itself whenever the wearer turns his wrist.

EARLY QUARTZ CLOCK

1930
Canadian-born American Warren Marrison invents the quartz clock. Powered by the regular vibrations of a quartz crystal in an electrical circuit, these clocks are highly accurate.

1949
Based on the vibration of atoms in ammonia molecules, the atomic clock is built by the U.S. National Bureau of Standards. Later models, containing cesium, hydrogen, or rubidium instead of ammonia, are accurate to within 1 second every 30 billion years.

1956
The digital clock is patented by an American, D. E. Protzmann. Digital wristwatches appear 14 years later.

1987
Voice-reactive watches are developed.

EARLY 1990s
Solar-powered digital watches are invented.

2000s
Watches can play music, record heart rate, show barometric

pressure, provide GPS, and alert the wearer to email notifications or phone calls. What's most important to remember, though, is that there will always be 24 hours in a day, 60 minutes in an hour, and 60 seconds in a minute. Use your time wisely!

THE TERM "WATCH" COMES FROM THE NIGHT WATCHMEN WHO CALLED OUT THE HOURS.

MAKE A TIME CAPSULE

A time capsule is a container into which historic records and special objects are deposited for preservation until a future date. Here's all you need to do:

1. Set a date for opening your capsule. Make it less than 50 years in the future, so that you can be fairly sure of being there.

2. Choose a capsule. If you plan to bury your container, it should be made of plastic, heavy-duty rubber, or metal. If it will remain indoors, plastic, wood, or metal will do. Make sure that the interior will stay cool, dry, and dark.

3. Fill your capsule. Select a variety of personal items: photos, DVDs, report cards, toys, jewelry, a restaurant menu (but not food!), tickets to an event you attended—things that relate to your life. Make a list of the contents. Put each item in a separate plastic bag for its protection.

4. Have a "sealing" ceremony. Invite your parents and friends. Take pictures, including a few of the capsule and its contents. Seal the capsule.

5. Store or bury the capsule. Keep it indoors where you can see it or, if you bury it, write down the location and keep that paper in a safe place. There are about 10,000 to 15,000 time capsules in the world, and most of them are lost. You do not want to forget where you put yours!

GHOSTLY TALES FOR

According to the records of the U.S. Coast Guard, hundreds, if not thousands, of ships have been wrecked over the years. Mystery surrounds many of them, including these.

HIDDEN IN PLAIN SIGHT

In the late 1880s, *Marlborough* left New Zealand for Great Britain. She was last reported near the Straits of Magellan. There, she vanished.

In 1913, the captain of a ship sailing off Tierra del Fuego stared hard at the green sea. It appeared that a huge, solid green lacework, having detached itself from the calm sea surface and risen upright, was now coming slowly toward him. Through his binoculars, the startled skipper saw a three-masted vessel. Its remaining sails were brilliant green. Its shrouds, decks, and superstructure were all the same bright emerald hue. The skipper called out. Failing to get a reply from the stranger, he set out in a small boat with some of his crew to investigate.

It was *Marlborough*—still afloat after 24 years. Her decks were pasty with decay. The crew had turned to skeletons slimy to the touch, yet with tatters of clothing clinging to them. The brilliant green that provided excellent camouflage was caused by the scum of algae gathered while drifting over countless miles in the ocean.

A HALLOWED EVE

ICED IN TIME

On April 6, 1951, in the north of Newfoundland, a member of a Canadian ship's crew reported a great iceberg some miles to the northeast. He told the captain that the floating mountain appeared to have eyes in its face. As the iceberg came closer, the captain focused his spyglass on a vast ledge about 200 feet up on the berg. He saw two complete ships standing upright. Their masts, hulls, and superstructures appeared undamaged. They rode the great frozen mass together, their bowsprits sharp in the same direction.

The captain could not read the ships' names, but from the general configuration they were thought to be the HMS *Terror* and HMS *Erebus,* the two lost ships of Sir John Franklin's last expedition of 1845. However, the two vessels and their true identity and contents could not be verified because the face of the iceberg was too steep to climb.

Some 63 years later, in September 2014, a Canadian expedition—using a remotely operated underwater vehicle—discovered the remains of the HMS *Erebus* in the eastern stretches of the Queen Maud Gulf, some 2,000 miles northwest of Newfoundland. The search for the HMS *Terror* continues.

CHASED IN A FOG

In a thick fog off the coast of France in 1884, the English collier *Rumney* ran her bow into the middle of the fine refrigerated French merchantman *Frigorifique.* The French crew leaped safely aboard *Rumney.* Soon after, with an extreme tilt to starboard and her gunwale awash, the stricken ship passed behind the curtain of fog.

Several hours later, as *Rumney*'s steam whistle shrieked over the water, *Frigorifique* came out of the fog with a rush, her stack billowing. On a series of rapid orders, *Rumney*'s powerful bow swung to meet the threat head on. But the merchantman swerved and stove in the collier's side, ruining the hold and engine room and opening the ship's vitals to the sea. Within minutes, the two crews were in the lifeboats and far enough away to watch the stocky *Rumney* sink amid columns of her own steam.

Again the *Frigorifique* went into hiding—although not for long. Once more, she came out of the mists with a rush and bore down upon the lifeboats. In a flurry of frenzied rowing, the men escaped by a few feet. With stretched nerves, they shivered and awaited the next unseen blow. But soon the fog lifted and, a couple of miles off, the *Frigorifique* could be seen sailing freely. She was moving in great circles, smoke still issuing high from her funnel, a faint propeller wake streaming from her stern.

Evidently, in the collision, the helm of the French ship's port side had become jammed hard. With slowly weakening boiler pressure but still moving at a good pace, the ship had made great circles that cut across the fog-draped paths of *Rumney* and, later, the lifeboats.

GET SHIPSHAPE

- **COLLIER:** a cargo ship for carrying coal
- **GUNWALE:** upper edge of the side of a boat or ship
- **HELM:** tiller or wheel or other equipment for steering a ship
- **HOLD:** area in a ship where cargo is stored
- **PORT AND STARBOARD:** the left side and right sides of a ship, respectively, when you are facing forward

A True "Captain Kid"

At 12 years old, he was the youngest officer in the U.S. Navy.

Cape Horn, at the southern tip of Chile and often fraught with raging seas and howling storms, has been the graveyard of many sailing ships. Yet, in the late 1700s and early 1800s, vessels continued to round the Horn because the Pacific Ocean was alive with whales. New England seamen spent long months at sea to bring home cargoes of whale oil for lamps and baleen (a stiff, flexible material from the whale's mouth) for buggy whips, carriage springs, corset stays and skirt hoops, fishing poles, and umbrella ribs.

Whaling was making America prosperous at the time, but this continued only until the beginning of hostilities with Great Britain during the War of 1812. Then American whaling ships lay idle at the docks or fell prey at sea to powerful British sailing warships or privateers. Many American ships, however, were still in the Pacific Ocean hunting grounds, and it was to protect these that Capt. David Porter took the frigate *Essex*, a sailing warship, around the angry Cape.

Ever vigilant, Porter and his crew captured several British ships that had taken possession of American whalers. He then released the American crews.

On board *Essex* was "Jimmy," a 12-year-old midshipman and son of a Spanish-American immigrant. He had been adopted by the captain's family and lived with them from the age of 7, soon after his own mother had died. Porter was like a father to him.

Unbeknownst to Porter, the whaler *Barclay* had sailed from New Bedford, Massachusetts, in 1811, under Capt. Gideon Randall. While off the coast of Peru, the *Barclay* had been captured by the Peruvian privateer ship *Nereyda.* (At the time, Peru was Britain's ally.) *Nereyda*'s captain removed Randall and his crew from the *Barclay* and put his own men aboard.

Soon after this takeover, Porter and *Essex* met and captured *Nereyda,* setting free Randall and his crew. *Barclay* was also recaptured.

Porter offered to return *Barclay*'s captain and crew to their own ship, but the crew refused to go. They felt safer aboard the well-armed *Essex.*

Instead, Porter chose U.S. Navy sailors from his own ship to crew *Barclay* and summoned Jimmy. "James," he said, "you've been with me in the Navy for 3 years now. You should know by this time how to command a ship."

The boy saluted and said, "Aye, aye, sir." Then Jimmy's eyes grew wide as he considered the captain's words: "Command a ship?" He was about to have one of the greatest adventures of his life.

Placing a hand on Jimmy's shoulder, Porter said, "I'm giving you

full command of *Barclay*. I want you to take her to Valparaiso, Chile, and meet me in the harbor there. Do you understand?"

Jimmy gulped as he saluted and answered, "Aye, aye, sir. I understand." He then glanced at Randall.

Porter turned to Randall and the Navy men chosen to be *Barclay*'s crew. He explained Jimmy's command. "You will take your orders from him," Porter told his sailors, and added: "I expect that Captain Randall will render whatever navigational or other services he may be called upon to perform."

Randall scowled and began to shake his fist. "Now, see here . . . !," he began.

"That's all, men," Porter said—and walked away.

As the sailors prepared to board the whaler, Porter smiled down at young Jimmy. "Don't worry. I have every confidence in you and your ability, or I wouldn't have given you this command. Have faith in God and in yourself, and you'll be all right, son."

"Thank you, sir," the boy said. "I'll do my best."

As *Barclay* prepared to leave the harbor, Randall walked over to Jimmy. "Boy," he said, "maybe Porter thinks you're going to Valparaiso with my ship, but if you ask me, you'll find yourself off New Zealand swimming with the sharks!"

Jimmy was a little scared. Standing about 4 feet 8 inches tall and weighing about 70 pounds, he felt tiny as he gazed up at the towering masts and the great sheets of canvas flapping in the breeze—and especially at the bearded face of Randall glaring down at him. But Jimmy was a midshipman in the Navy and he had a mission to perform.

Randall held back his words, went to the ship's rail, and stood looking out over the sea. Jimmy decided to try to make friends with him. The boy went to the rail and stood beside him.

"Captain Randall," Jimmy said, "do you think we should fill away the main topsail? We're not making—"

Randall turned swiftly and snapped: "We'll not fill the main topsail or any other sail without my orders!" He straightened up and cried out, "I'm the master of this ship and I'll shoot any man that lays a hand on a sail or a line without my orders!"

Some of the sailors were watching and listening, but none moved. Randall poked a finger into Jimmy's chest. "I'll chart my own course," he said. "I'm not trusting myself to any confounded, wet-nosed brat!"

He started to walk away, but then stopped abruptly and turned to face Jimmy again. "You heard me, boy!" He roared. "I'm going below to get my pistols. You'd better think twice before you give an order on this ship." He strode off, muttering to himself.

Jimmy saw the sailors watching him. He looked up at the white clouds floating beneath the deep blue sky, and he remembered the words of Porter: "Have faith in God and yourself . . . ." Trying to be calm, he held up one hand and called to his first officer. The officer approached him and saluted.

"Fill the main topsail!" Jimmy said.

The officer saluted again. "Aye, aye, sir!" Then he turned and shouted the command to the crew.

As Jimmy saw his order being carried out, he grew confident. He was in the right. He went below to Randall's quarters and knocked on the door. Randall opened it.

"Captain Randall," Jimmy said quietly, "if you come on deck with your pistols, I shall have you thrown over the side. That's all, Captain Randall." He walked away.

Randall never brought out his pistols, and Jimmy took *Barclay* safely to Valparaiso, where he rejoined Porter. Three days later, Jimmy celebrated his 12th birthday.

DID YOU KNOW?

So close was the relationship between Capt. David Porter and Jimmy that the young midshipman later changed his first name from James to David.

David Glasgow Farragut—yes, our Jimmy—grew up to become the first vice admiral, rear admiral, and full admiral in the U.S. Navy.

BRING ON BREAKFAST!

You've probably heard that breakfast is the most important meal of the day. Know why?

Think of your body as a machine. Its engine runs even when you are asleep. After running for 8 to 10 hours without any fuel (food), your body needs a refill. That's why we eat breakfast.

Even if you are not hungry in the morning, eating a small meal or a piece of fruit is better than eating nothing. Without breakfast, you may feel sluggish and grumpy all morning—and that's no fun.

A healthy breakfast helps to improve your performance in school and gives you energy to help you concentrate in class.

Try these fun and yummy ideas to get you going in the morning. Bet you never skip breakfast again!

ASK A PARENT TO HELP, IF NECESSARY, AND MAKE ENOUGH FOR HIM OR HER, TOO!

ENGLISH MUFFIN DELIGHT

The combinations are endless! Try them all.

1 English muffin
2 to 3 tablespoons cream cheese, Greek yogurt, or peanut butter
fresh fruit, such as blueberries and/or sliced strawberries, peaches, or bananas
honey, for drizzling (optional)

1. Slice English muffin in half. Toast (in toaster) to desired doneness.

2. Spread each half with cream cheese. Top with fruit. Drizzle honey on top (if using).

Makes 1 serving.

BANANA PANCAKES

Freeze any leftovers, and when you want fast food, pop one in the toaster.

1½ cups buttermilk
1 cup mashed, ripe bananas
3 tablespoons unsalted butter, melted
1 tablespoon lemon juice
2 eggs, beaten
1½ cups all-purpose flour
2 tablespoons sugar
1½ teaspoons baking powder
½ teaspoon baking soda
½ teaspoon salt

1. In a bowl, combine buttermilk, bananas, butter, lemon juice, and eggs.

2. In another bowl, combine flour, sugar, baking powder, baking soda, and salt.

3. Add dry ingredients to wet ingredients and mix well. Let rest for 5 minutes.

4. Preheat a griddle and coat with nonstick cooking spray. Sprinkle with drops of water. If the water drops jump around, the griddle is ready.

5. Pour batter using a ¼ cup measure. Flip pancakes when puffed and full of bubbles. Cook for 2 to 3 minutes, or until bottom is golden brown.

Makes 12 to 14 pancakes.

Convert to metric on p. 181

GRANOLA

Use any kind of dried fruit: apricots, pineapple, raisins—whatever you like.

2 cups old-fashioned oats
⅓ cup unsweetened shredded coconut (optional)
½ cup slivered or whole almonds
½ teaspoon sea salt
2 tablespoons honey
2 tablespoons pure maple syrup
2 tablespoons brown sugar
2 tablespoons (¼ stick) unsalted butter
½ teaspoon pure vanilla extract
½ cup dried cranberries
½ cup dried cherries
milk or yogurt, for serving

1. Preheat oven to 325°F. Line a rimmed baking sheet with parchment paper.

2. In a large bowl, combine oats, coconut (if using), almonds, and salt.

3. In a saucepan over medium heat, combine honey, maple syrup, brown sugar, butter, and vanilla. Bring to a boil (but don't let it boil over). Reduce heat and simmer for 5 minutes, stirring often.

4. Pour hot honey mixture over oat mixture and stir to coat. Spread evenly on prepared baking sheet.

5. Bake for 15 minutes, stirring occasionally. Add cranberries and cherries and stir.

6. Bake for 15 minutes more, stirring occasionally, until golden brown.

7. Cool completely. Serve with milk or yogurt or eat dry.

Granola will keep in an airtight container at room temperature for up to 2 weeks.

Makes about 3½ cups.

BREAKFAST PIZZA

Pizza for breakfast? Yes, please!

refrigerated pizza dough
4 eggs, beaten
1 cup shredded cheddar cheese
½ cup cooked, chopped bacon or cooked sausage crumbles
6 cherry tomatoes, sliced (optional)

1. Preheat oven to 400°F. Spray a round pizza pan with nonstick cooking spray.

2. Place dough on prepared pan. Press out dough until it reaches the edge of the pan. Bake for about 8 minutes, or until crust is lightly golden.

3. In a pan over medium heat, cook eggs, stirring frequently, until firm but not dry. Spread on pizza crust. Sprinkle cheddar, bacon, and tomatoes (if using) on top of eggs.

4. Bake for 10 to 12 minutes, or until crust is golden brown and cheese is melted. Cut into six equal slices.

Makes 6 servings.

PB&B SMOOTHIE

Always keep a banana in the freezer.

¾ cup low-fat milk
½ cup ice cubes (4 or 5)
2 tablespoons peanut butter*
½ frozen banana
***If you are allergic to peanuts, substitute sunflower butter.**

Combine all ingredients in a blender and process until smooth.

Makes 1 serving.

MOUTHFULS OF FUN!

Convert to metric on p. 181

With a little imagination, you can turn everyday food into fun snacks, party treats, and good-for-you nibbles. Invite your friends over to make these or surprise your family by serving up something extraordinary!

CUPCAKE CONES

No melt, no mess, and fun to make

1 box of your favorite cake mix
24 plain ice cream cones with flat bottoms
1 container (16 ounces) of your favorite frosting
chocolate or rainbow sprinkles

1. Preheat oven to 350°F.

2. Prepare cake mix according to package directions. (Ask an adult to help, if necessary.)

3. Place 1 cone into each cup of a 12-cup muffin tin. Repeat with another muffin tin. Pour or spoon batter into cones, filling each about two-thirds full. Bake for 20 minutes, or until a toothpick inserted into the center of a cone comes out clean. Set aside to cool.

4. Frost each cupcake cone. Decorate with sprinkles.

Makes 24 cupcake cones.

WATERMELON PIZZA

A slice is nice, and two are good for you!

1 large watermelon

fruit such as kiwi, orange, pineapple, and strawberries, cut up, plus blueberries and/or blackberries

unsweetened shredded coconut (optional)

1. Cut a full-round slice from the middle of the watermelon. (Ask an adult to help, if necessary.) If desired, cut another full-round slice to make another pizza. Save the remaining watermelon to eat later.

2. Place a watermelon round on a serving platter. Top with fruit. Sprinkle with coconut (if using).

3. Using a pizza cutter, slice the watermelon pizza into six equal pieces.

Makes 6 servings.

CANDY CORN GELATIN CUPS

No tricks, just treats! Be sure to plan ahead. This takes time.

1 package (3.4 ounces) vanilla instant pudding
1 cup hot water
1 package (3 ounces) orange-flavor gelatin
1 cup cold water
1½ cups whipped cream or frozen dessert topping, thawed
candy corn pieces

1. Prepare pudding according to package directions. Pour or spoon a layer of pudding into 4 to 6 (depending on size) clear (see-through) dessert cups. Refrigerate.

2. In a bowl, mix hot water and gelatin. Stir until gelatin is completely dissolved. Pour in cold water and stir. Refrigerate for 30 minutes, or until slightly thickened.

3. Remove dessert cups from refrigerator. Spoon a layer of gelatin over pudding. Return to refrigerator for at least 1 hour.

4. When ready to serve, top with whipped cream. Decorate with candy corn.

Makes 4 to 6 servings.

GRAPE SNAKES

. . . for a most healthy snack attack

2 wooden skewers
10 green grapes
10 red grapes
cream cheese, softened
4 miniature chocolate chips

1. Push green grapes onto 1 skewer, then push red grapes onto the other. (Or, alternate putting red and green grapes on the same skewer. Repeat—green, red, green, red, etc., until you get to 10.)

2. Put a spoonful of cream cheese into the corner of a plastic sandwich bag. Using scissors, cut off the tip of the corner of the bag. Squeeze 2 cream cheese eyes onto the first grape on each skewer. Press chocolate chips (eyes) into the cream cheese.

Makes 2 servings.

BANANA DOG

The peel deal!

1 hot dog bun
2 tablespoons peanut butter, plus extra for topping*
2 tablespoons jelly, plus extra for topping
1 banana, peeled

*If you are allergic to peanut butter, substitute sunflower butter.

1. Open hot dog bun and spread peanut butter on one side. Spread jelly on other side. Put banana in center of bun and add more peanut butter and jelly, as desired.

Makes 1 serving.

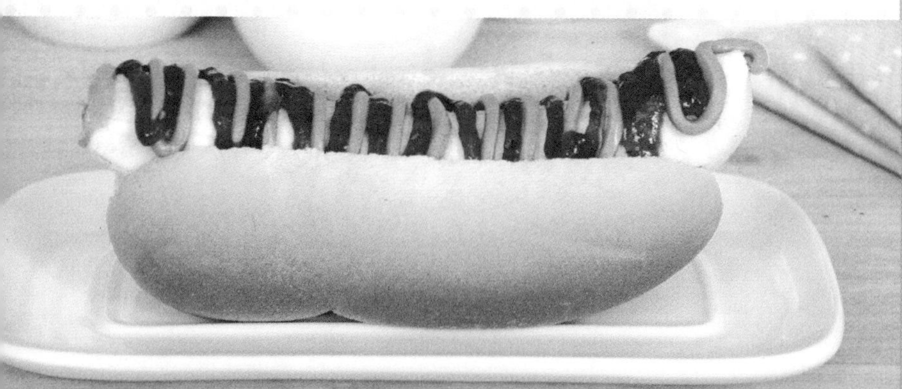

THE CASE FOR A

They're lovable little creatures—and probably something that none of your friends has!

Crickets are easy to manage, sing in a way that you'll love, and don't eat much. What's not to like?

A field cricket is shiny-black or brown, with brown wings. A fully grown cricket is a bit less than an inch long. Males and females are easy to tell apart, and telling them apart is vital if you want one for a pet, because the female does not sing. At his rear, the male has two thin, pronglike sensory organs. The female has three prongs, the middle and longest one being her ovipositor, with which she injects eggs into the soil. Don't confuse crickets with grasshoppers. A cricket is shorter and stubbier than a grasshopper and stays close to

PET CRICKET

the ground. The cricket won't jump, except in desperation.

In the fall, the female cricket lays her eggs (up to 400!) in the ground. They hatch in the spring, producing thousands of tiny black field crickets swarming in the tall grass. These moult rapidly, and by the time the males are large enough to start singing in late July or early August, they have become not only bigger, but also more cautious. Each male selects a den to which he can retreat at a moment's notice—this can be a tiny hole in the ground, a crack in a cement wall, a crevice under a piece of bark—and begins to sing.

Unlike the grasshopper, the cricket doesn't sing by rubbing his legs together. He lifts his wing casings at a 45-degree angle and rubs them together—one has toothlike ridges (called the "file") and the other has a hardened edge (called the "scraper"). Imagine rubbing your thumb against the teeth of a comb to get the idea.

The cricket sings to attract a mate. But in captivity, he will also sing when you give him food (crickets can eat and sing at the same time). Some crickets become so tame that they will sing when you blow gently on them—they seem to like the warmth. Like all insects, crickets are cold-blooded, and they sing faster or slower depending on the temperature.

We've observed that a cricket's song is territorial. One fall, we recorded a cricket's song on tape. When the recording was played across the room, he showed no interest. But when it was placed near his cage, he went wild, clawing at the sides to get at his rival. After a few more tries, placing the tape player at different distances, we determined his territory to be about 2 feet in diameter.

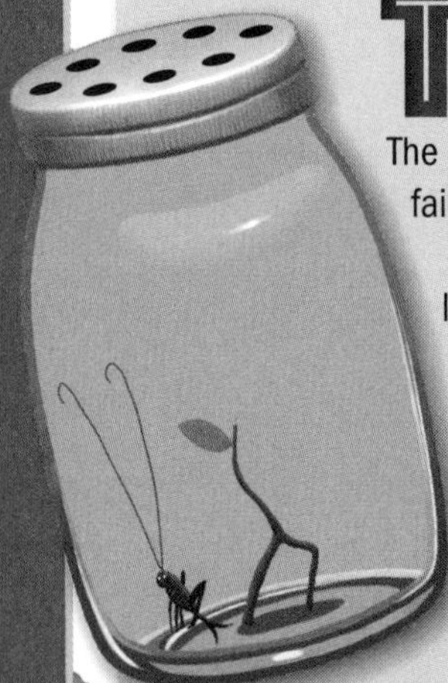

The best cricket house is a medium-size pickle jar with holes punched in the lid. By far the worst home for a pet cricket is a cute sandalwood and bamboo cricket cage. The cricket squeezes himself between the bars to escape or, failing that, simply chews through the bamboo.

After you get your cricket, add sand or clean soil and leaves to the bottom of its container. A piece of bark makes him feel more at home. If a pickle jar is not available, you could put him into a fishbowl or terrarium bottle. The top must be covered tightly with wire mesh, but there are no guarantees that your cricket will not escape. Even with mesh, they can still sometimes squeeze underneath the edge (and they can hurt themselves in trying). They're safer under a ventilated screw top.

Convert to metric on p. 181

Now comes the hard part: the hunt. Crickets abound in fields and front lawns, but the minute you get to within a few feet of a cricket, he goes quiet and retreats into a hole. The best place to catch him is on your own turf. In the fall, crickets often come inside, attracted by the warmth. Anytime you hear one singing in a bathroom or a cellar, there is a potentially easy catch.

Once you're pretty sure that you have a cricket in your hand, be careful. Their legs and antennae can break off, and they can bite like crazy. If you're outside and your pickle jar is sitting on the shelf miles away, the next best thing is a cotton handkerchief. Wrap him loosely so that he won't suffocate and try to get him home as soon as possible.

The best place to transfer the cricket to his jar is the bathtub. A newly caught cricket will make desperate attempts to escape. Close the tub drain and shower curtains—a glass-enclosed shower stall would be ideal. After he becomes tame, you can put him safely into another jar while you clean the old one by tipping it up. He will slide down the glass.

Once he is safely in the jar, be careful about using insect sprays. They can kill him as well as harmful insects. He needs both food and water every day. For water, the most convenient dish is the lid of a plastic pill container. It can be put into the jar with tweezers and filled by drawing and releasing water through a straw. The water dish should be cleaned and refilled every day.

Crickets will eat almost anything, including your woolens, if they escape. They like cereals of all kinds: cornflakes, oats, granola. They are crazy about birdseed, especially sunflower seeds, and will also eat apple peelings, lettuce, raw carrots, and other raw vegetables. It's best to go easy on the food. They eat very little; any food should be removed every day, so that the jar does not grow moldy. Clean the jar and put in fresh dirt every 2 or 3 days.

Now we come to the sad part. A cricket's life span is very short. Outdoors, the first frost kills the crickets, but even in a warm house with good care, they don't last through the winter. If you catch one in good condition in August or September, it should last until Thanksgiving.

Sometimes you will find the cricket lifeless in the morning. Sometimes they seem to lose their balance and flop about—when this happens, put them outdoors. Occasionally, on one night their song just gets fainter and fainter, like that of Tinker Bell in *Peter Pan,* until it fades away by dawn. When this time comes, say good-bye to your cricket and leave him in the grass. Give the jar a good washing and put it away for next fall.

DID YOU KNOW?

- Crickets have been prized as pets in Japan and China for centuries.
- In China, cricket fighting was once popular. Two crickets were put in a pottery jar. They would fight regardless of whether a female was present, and they fought fiercely, losing legs and antennae, often to the death. So it's best not to keep two males together.
- A cricket's ears are located on its front legs.
- Crickets are found all over the world. At least 120 species exist in North America.

CALCULATE THE CHIRP-ERATURE

Crickets rub their wings together to produce chirps. The speed with which they rub them depends on the temperature of the air. By counting the chirps, you can figure out the approximate temp.

- **For the temperature in Fahrenheit, count the chirps in 14 seconds and add 40. Example: 48 chirps + 40 = 88°F.**
- **For the temperature in Celsius, count the chirps in 25 seconds, divide by 3, then add 4. Example: (48 chirps ÷ 3) + 4 = 20°C.**

READY TO PLAY?

Cricket is a match (not a game) played on a pitch (not a field) by sides (or teams) dressed in whites, with batsmen (not batters) striking a ball thrown by a bowler (not a pitcher) whose delivery (not throw) must be executed overhand. A poor batsman is called a "rabbit," a really poor batsman is called a "ferret," and a batsman who pinch hits is called a "night watchman."

The first match played in North America before a public audience took place in 1751. The first international sporting event in the modern world was a match between the United States and Canada in 1844. Today, cricket is played in more than 92 countries around the world.

ANIMAL HEROES

More ways and reasons to love our pets

THE NOSE KNOWS

Luke, age 7, and his dog, Jedi, are pals, buddies, best friends. Luke is diabetic, and Jedi is his Diabetic Alert Dog. Jedi is trained to use his nose to detect when Luke's health is at risk and then alert an adult.

Late one night, Luke was asleep in a bed near his mother. Jedi was also nearby. Without his knowing it, Luke's blood sugar level dropped—a danger to someone with diabetes. Jedi smelled the change in Luke's breath and sprang into action. He jumped on and off the bed to wake Luke's mother. When this didn't work, he laid his body on top of hers. This woke her up. Then Jedi bowed; that's his way of saying that Luke's blood sugar is "low." Luke's mother was then able to care for him.

CAT IN THE BOX

Masha is a stray cat. Her long, thick hair keeps her warm during the bitterly cold winters, and many neighbors feed her as she roams the streets.

One frigid night, Masha spotted a cardboard box in the chilly hallway of an apartment building. In the box was a tiny baby! The infant boy was dressed—but not well enough to protect him from the cold. Masha climbed inside the box and cuddled the child. Her warm body kept him comfortable and alive. Several hours later, when someone heard the baby cry, he was discovered and rushed to a hospital.

KIDS CAN BE HEROES TO PETS, TOO!

Daisy the dog was homeless, dirty, and hungry when she arrived at the animal shelter. After being washed and fed, she was put into a kennel. Daisy had always run free, but now she was alone in a tiny room. She crouched in the corner, shivering with fear.

One day, Daisy heard a child's voice and perked up her ears. A little girl was sitting beside her kennel, reading a book out loud. The more the girl read, the less Daisy shook. After a few minutes, Daisy crept closer to the edge of her kennel. By the time the girl had finished reading the story, Daisy had relaxed and crept as close to the girl as she could.

Some time later, a family arrived to adopt a dog. Daisy bravely came to the front of her kennel to see who it was. She wagged her clean, fluffy tail and won the hearts of the family. Now she has a loving home. Kids who read to shelter dogs help the dogs to calm down. As a result, the dogs are adopted more quickly.

KHAN DO

When a young family went to the animal shelter to adopt a pet, they did not know how important their choice would be. The family immediately befriended Khan, a Doberman Pinscher that had been abused. Khan seemed to like them, and he was the same height as the family's 17-month-old daughter, Charlotte.

Four days later, as Khan watched Charlotte play in the yard, he suddenly sensed danger. A large, poisonous snake was slithering toward the girl. Khan tried to push Charlotte away, but she wouldn't budge. Just as the snake was about to strike the child, Khan gripped his teeth on Charlotte's diaper and tossed her about 3 feet to safety. The snake instead bit Khan's paw! The family rushed him to a vet, who gave the dog an antivenom shot that enabled him to soon recover.

FIRE ALARM

Patience the cat didn't have much patience early one morning in 2015. As her family slept, smoke began filling their house in Loyalsock Township, Pennsylvania. The kitchen was on fire! Patience jumped onto her owners' bed and yowled to wake the family. It worked! Everyone escaped safely thanks to impatient Patience.

Convert to metric on p. 181

OH, RATS!

African pouched rats can spread diseases and destroy crops, so some people jump to conclusions and think bad things about Henry, a 2½-pound African pouched—that is, until they learn how useful Henry and his friends can be.

Henry and other African pouched rats are being trained to smell TNT, which is contained in land mines. (Land mines are set in the ground during wars. Many innocent people have been hurt when they have stepped unknowingly on hidden mines and exploded them.) The rats' job is to run into a field and sniff for TNT. They don't weigh enough to set off the pressure-sensitive mines. When a rat smells the explosive, it scratches the spot where it is buried. The trainer, who holds the animal on a leash, marks the spot for professionals who will later remove the mine and then gives the rat a treat.

In 1 hour, Henry can locate more mines than a human with a metal detector can in a day. Every tasty treat that Henry and his buddies earn saves lives.

FOR THE LOVE OF TENNIS

ONCE A GAME FOR KINGS,
TENNIS TODAY IS FUN FOR EVERYBODY.

SPORTS

The Final Tie will be Played on Monday, July 16, at 3.30 p.m.

LAWN TENNIS CHAMPIONSHIP,
OPEN TO ALL AMATEURS.

FIRST PRIZE.—The GOLD CHAMPION PRIZE, value 12 guineas, with a Silver Challenge Cup, value 25 guineas (presented by the Proprietors of *The Field*).
SECOND PRIZE.—The SILVER PRIZE, value 7 guineas.
THIRD PRIZE.—Value 3 guineas.

Tennis dates from the 12th and 13th centuries, when monks and kings in France began hitting a ball with bare hands against a wall. They called it *jeu de paume* (game of the palm). Eventually, the idea caught on, and players began to hit the ball over a net using gloves and, later, racquets. In 1877, the All England Croquet and Lawn Tennis Club in Wimbledon, England, sponsored their first tennis championship and established the rules and regulations that are used today.

BOUNCING THROUGH TIME

THE EVOLUTION OF TENNIS EQUIPMENT AND COURTS . . .

Early tennis balls were made of hair, wool, or cork wrapped into a ball and covered with cloth or leather.

Eventually, players who wore a **glove** to protect their hand added netting between the glove's fingers.

Some players used a **solid paddle.** Webbing, usually made from sheep or cow gut, was woven into the paddle, making it more like the tennis racquet we know today.

TENNIS TALK

Ace: a serve that the opponent does not return

Doubles: a match with teams of two people

Game: a sequence of points (0–15–30–40–game)

Let: a shot that is replayed (such as when a serve touches the net)

Lob: a shot hit high above the net

Love: a score of zero. Some believe that this is because a zero is shaped like an egg and in French, the word for "the egg" is *l'oeuf,* which evolved into "love."

Match: a contest between two people or teams; usually three or five sets

Rally: a series of hits between players after a serve

Set: six games

Volley: a shot hit by the receiver before it bounces in his/her court

Convert to metric on p. 181

Early tennis courts were hourglass-shape—narrower at the net and wider at each end. (Today's courts are rectangular and measure 78 feet long by 27 feet wide.)

In 1844, Charles Goodyear invented **rubber,** which bounced better on grass courts (where the game was called lawn tennis).

In 1887, **Lottie Dod,** at 15 the youngest-ever Wimbledon ladies' singles champion, wore a calf-length white dress and black stockings. White is still preferred for tennis outfits today. In the 1930s, men and women began wearing shorts and tops.

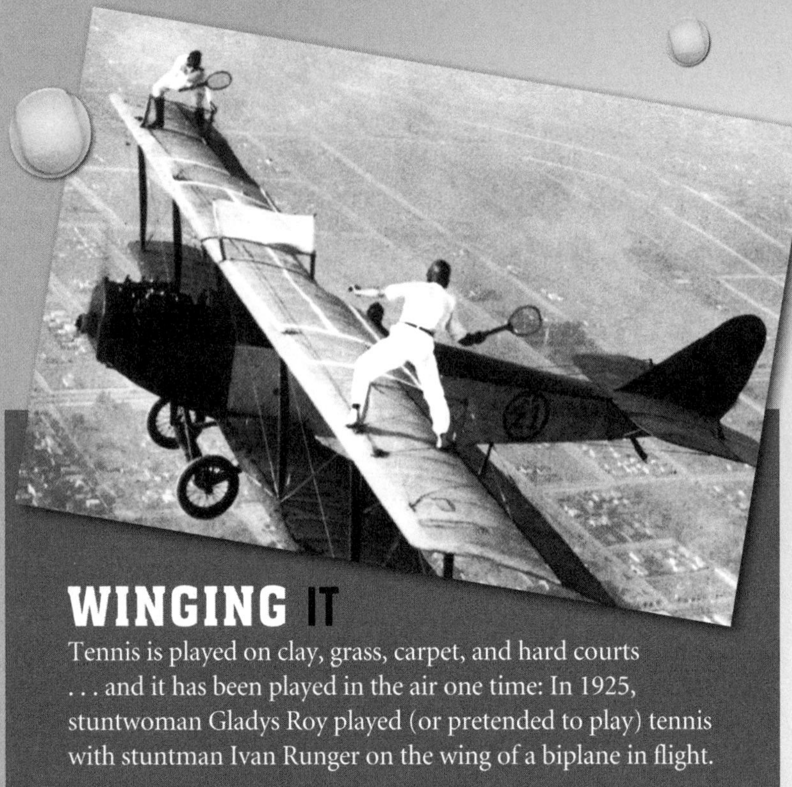

WINGING IT

Tennis is played on clay, grass, carpet, and hard courts . . . and it has been played in the air one time: In 1925, stuntwoman Gladys Roy played (or pretended to play) tennis with stuntman Ivan Runger on the wing of a biplane in flight.

GOT GAME? GET INTO ACTION

You don't have to be a great athlete to enjoy the fun and health benefits of tennis. Check out your local courts, recreation department, or schools for information about clubs and informal gatherings of potential players with all skill levels.

Like many sports, tennis requires strength, speed, endurance, and good hand-eye coordination.

- **If you need to, jog and do push-ups and sit-ups to help get into shape.**
- **Practice "dribbles" to improve your hand-eye coordination. See how many times in a row you can bounce the ball off the ground with your racquet. Or, count how many times you can bounce the ball off your racquet while keeping it off the ground. Try to improve your score the next time you practice.**

TWO-WHEEL WONDERS

In 1976, after 18-year-old Brad Parks suffered a skiing accident that left his legs paralyzed, he created a new sport—wheelchair tennis. Players use specially designed wheelchairs that move easily and fast on the court. The court and rules are the same as for able-bodied players, with one exception: A shot can bounce twice (not once) before it must be returned.

Wheelchair tennis is recognized by the International Tennis Foundation, and competitions are often played alongside major tournaments, with divisions for juniors, men, and women.

ANIMALS AT COURT

- Officials at the All England Lawn and Tennis Club in Wimbledon have a unique way of keeping the court free of birds that may interrupt the game—or worse, leave unwanted droppings. Since 2007, Rufus, a Harris hawk trained by Wayne and Imogen Davis, has visited each week to discourage pigeons from roosting. During each visit, Rufus flies around for about 1 hour—just long enough to let other birds know that he's the boss. Imogen is training a new hawk, Pollux, to take over when Rufus retires. In trial flights, Pollux often lands on the TV camera. But with Rufus's help, Imogen expects that Pollux will soon be able to patrol on his own.
- In 1854, in England, a tennis ball in play hit and killed a sparrow. Three other birds are reported to have been hit and killed during the Australian Open, most recently in 2016.
- In a 1949 Wimbledon match, a squirrel brought the game to a stop for 3 minutes as it scurried around the court, looking for an escape route.

Get Out Your Clams,

It's "game on" for keepsies!

Playing marbles—flicking, or shooting, small colored glass balls on or into a target area—is a very old pastime. Exactly where and when the game of marbles began is not known. Archaeologists have dug up small clay and stone balls in caves in Europe and in Egyptian tombs. Ancient Romans played using round nuts and called it Nuts! (Well, translated it was "Nuts.")

Glass marbles were first manufactured in Germany in the mid-1800s. The first North American marbles were made from clay around 1884. They became known as "commies" because they were the most common kind of marbles.

Today's marbles come in many sizes and colors. Glass marbles often show swirls of different colors.

Peewees, and Taws!

How to Shoot

Make a loose fist with the fingers of your dominant hand, except your thumb. Put your shooter—a larger-than-ordinary marble—against the ball of your pointer finger. Put your thumbnail behind it. Flick your thumb to propel the marble forward.

Some games insist on all or a couple of knuckles on the ground when shooting (you have to be on your knees); others allow no knuckles on the ground. Decide with your friends how you want to play.

Games

There are many games and many ways to play marbles, and some games have many different names. Learn these three games, then make up your own.

- ARCHBOARD: Players shoot marbles into box cutouts.
- RINGER: Players knock marbles out of a circle
- POTSIE: Players shoot marbles into a hole.

Before you begin, agree among yourselves on whether you are playing "for fair," in which all marbles are returned to the owners, or "for keeps" or "keepsies," in which the winner takes all the marbles. Beginners usually play "for fair."

Archboard

You will need a shoebox or tissue box. With scissors, cut arches (curved or square) of different sizes (big enough for marbles to pass through) into the long edge of the box (not the bottom). Above each arch, write a number. (The more difficult shots should have higher numbers.) Place the box upside down on the playing surface.

Decide how many marbles each player will use.

The object is to a shoot marble at the box to get it through an arch. When your marble goes into one of the holes, you score points. The game is over when all of the marbles have been used. The player with the most points wins.

Ringer

Draw a large circle, 5 to 10 feet across, on the ground. Use chalk on a sidewalk or driveway; if you are playing indoors, use fine string to make a circle on the floor. In the center, place 13 marbles, spaced about 3 inches apart, to form an X.

Each player uses a designated shooter marble. The shooter marbles should all be of the same size and material. Players take turns shooting (or flicking) from anywhere outside the ring, trying to knock a target marble out of it, while keeping their shooter marble inside the ring.

OUTCOMES

- **If the shooter marble misses a target, the player picks up his shooter marble and his turn is over.**
- **If the shooter marble knocks a target out of the ring but the shooter marble also rolls out of the ring, the player keeps any marbles that rolled out, including his shooter, and his turn is over.**
- **If the shooter marble knocks a target out of the ring and stays inside the ring, the player shoots again from the spot where his shooter marble came to a stop. The player keeps any marbles that rolled out.**

The game ends when there are no more marbles inside the ring. The person who collects the most marbles is the winner.

Potsie

A hole (also called a "pot") is dug with the heel of a shoe, a simple utensil, or a shovel. A shallow hole is called a saucer.

Mark off a starting line a few feet away from the hole. Players attempt to shoot a marble into the hole. Whoever gets their marble into the hole wins. (It's like miniature golf.) If no player gets a marble into the hole during the first round, the players shoot again, starting with the marble farthest from the hole.

Marvelous Marbles

Marbles can be fancy or plain, different sizes and different materials. Learn these terms and you'll sound like a mibster!

AGGIE: a marble made of agate or a glass marble that looks like it is agate

ALLEY: a marble made of alabaster

CLAMS: marbles

CLAYEY: a marble made of clay

DEAD DUCK: an easy shot

DUBS: knocking two marbles out with one shot

KEEPSIES: playing for ownership of players' marbles

KNUCKLE DOWN: to put one knuckle of your shooting hand in contact with the ground.

LAGGING: choosing who shoots first. Players roll their marbles toward a line in the dirt (the lag line). The player who gets his marble closest to the line starts the game.

MIBS: target marbles

MIBSTER: marble game player

PEERIE OR PURIE: small clear glass marble

PEEWEE: a very small marble

STEELIE: a steel marble

TAW: a shooter marble

TRIPS: a shot in play that touches three marbles

Did You Know?

- Presidents George Washington, Thomas Jefferson, John Quincy Adams, and Abraham Lincoln were known to play marbles. It is said that Lincoln played marbles during the Civil War to relieve stress.
- Today, people of all ages compete in national and world championships. Girls were not allowed to participate in national marble tournaments until 1948.
- Handmade sulphides are clear glass marbles with white or silvery figures (animals, birds, or humans) suspended in the center. One of the most valuable of these, made for a political campaign, contains images of President James Garfield and his vice president, Chester Arthur.
- In Syria and Turkey, people play marbles with the knucklebones of sheep.

Have You Lost Your Marbles?

Years ago, marbles were highly prized. When a person misplaced something very important or special or did something outrageous, people would ask,"Have you lost your marbles?," meaning "Have you lost your wits or mind?"

A BIG WEIGHT ON

Pulling-horse teams love to work together

Horse pulling is a popular event at county fairs and special contests across the land. Pairs of draft horses compete to see which can pull the greatest weight on a heavy sledge across a short distance. The winners get prizes—blue ribbons, money, trophies, or maybe just an extra apple or two.

Pulling horses are far different from saddle horses and racehorses. Draft horses (from the Old English word *dragan,* meaning "to draw or haul") are much taller, heavier, and more muscular. They have been bred to help in plowing, hauling hay, and performing other heavy work around the farm

THEIR SHOULDERS

so much, they're ready to get hitched!

and in the woods.

Many of today's top pulling horses do not work on a farm. Like athletes, they get special training to enable strong and limber muscles and tendons; the best in grain, hay, and vitamins; and health, hoof, and grooming care to keep them in top condition.

The horses are excited at every competition. As pulling time nears, they are fed, watered, and groomed carefully. Then their trainers put specially fitted collars and harnesses on them, making them a true team. The horses can "feel" and hear the anticipation of the audience. They love pulling!

Convert to metric on p. 181

Standing behind the team, the driver ("teamster") holds the long reins, while a helper on each side holds one end of a bar called a whiffletree, with a hook in the middle, that is attached to the harnesses.

The teamster and helpers guide the team into the pit in front of the audience. The horses prance and strain, eager to begin pulling. The team is led to the front of the sledge, on which is a weight load—usually large blocks of concrete that were stacked by power equipment. Most competitions start at about 2,000 pounds.

Slowly, carefully, the horsemen back up the powerful animals until the helpers are able to "make the hitch," or drop the bar's hook onto a ring on the sledge.

When the horses hear the hook dropping onto the ring and sense that the helpers have let go of the bar, they start pulling—and the competition begins!

The horses pull with all their might, *pushing* their shoulders against their collars. The traditional pulling distance is 27 feet 6 inches. Occasionally, the teamster might tap them with the reins to encourage them. After a Herculean effort, they stop when they can go no farther or when the finish is sounded or the teamster commands them to.

The teams take turns as more weight is added in each round. When a team can not pull a round's weight the full distance, it is eliminated. When no team can pull the weight the full distance, the event is finished. The team that has pulled the final weight the farthest is declared the winner.

TEAM TALK

HITCH (NOUN): a pulling team ("Big Bob and Mighty Mike are a powerful hitch.")

HITCH (VERB): to make the connection between horses and sledge

PIT: the dirt area where the teams are attached to the sledge

RAIL: the edge of the pulling pit; going outside it disqualifies the team

SLEDGE: a heavy (usually) wooden sled with thick runners

STONE-BOAT: another name for the sledge, named after the sleds that farmers once used to haul stones out of fields

TEAMSTER: driver

WHIFFLETREE: the horizontal bar at the end of the horses' harnesses

"OH, YEAH?"

Horse pulling (also known as "horse drawing") probably began when one farmer said to another, "My team is better than yours," and the other responded, "Oh, yeah? Prove it!"

NO HORSIN' AROUND

Horse pulls are regularly supervised by state and provincial agricultural departments, fair commissioners, and animal welfare organizations.

TEAM WORK

The most common draft horses in pulls are the Belgian, Percheron, Clydesdale, and Shire breeds. Teams work best when the horses are the same size; if they are not, their harnesses and whiffletree bars can be adjusted to give the bigger horse a larger share of the load. Says one teamster: "Teams need to be a team, not just two good horses hitched together. It helps if one is a leader and the other is a little bit of a follower."

SUPER PULLERS!

One of the most successful teams has been Spongebob and Harley, handsome Percherons from Cromwell, Kentucky. At one competition in Florida in 2016, they pulled 4,500 pounds a distance of 19 feet 5 inches.

A LOT OF PULL

Horses are not the only work animals to pull competitively. Oxen, mules, and even dogs participate in their own pulling contests. All are subject to the same requirements of humane treatment as horse pulls.

Want to Set a WORLD RECORD?

TAKE THIS ADVICE FROM THE MAN WHO HOLDS THE MOST

Ashrita Furman is like nobody else on Earth. He holds more records in the *Guinness Book of World Records* than anyone else (even *that's* a record), and he has his own category in the collection. As of 2014, Ashrita had set 551 official records since he began setting them in 1979.

How does he do it? What are his secrets?

Ashrita offers some tips for success based on his past experience. Study them carefully. He knows what he's talking about.

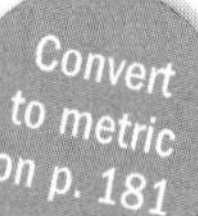
Convert to metric on p. 181

GET MOTIVATED

It helps to undertake a challenge. For Ashrita, a self-described former wimp from Queens, New York, it was a bike race. For 24 hours, he rode around Central Park along with thousands of other bikers. He pedaled 405 miles, coming in third overall—a remarkable feat, especially because he had hardly trained.

Ashrita credits his success to determination and meditation. The bike race was a challenge, and it was only the beginning.

AMUSEMENT

Ashrita Furman

CHOOSE A RECORDABLE ACTIVITY

Early in his record-breaking career, Ashrita juggled 100,000 times in a row in Grand Central Station. The event drew an admiring crowd. He submitted his record to the Guinness book, only to find that they wouldn't accept it because the category didn't exist.

The lesson: Stick to the established categories.

Know the Rules

Ashrita's second attempt to get into the Guinness book involved a pogo stick. Challenging himself to set the record for the most continuous pogo stick jumps, he completed 100,000 jumps in 13 hours—a record—and then continued for 24 hours, taking occasional rests every hour.

Only afterward did he learn that his rests were longer than the legal time allowed. The record was invalidated.

DO WHAT YOU LOVE

Ashrita set his favorite record in Japan, pogo-sticking up and down the foothills of Mount Fuji for 11½ miles. "Someone eventually broke my record on flat land: They did 12 miles. But I did 13 miles and broke it right back again," says Ashrita.

On the other hand, the record for continuous clapping just wasn't worth defending. "I clapped for 50 hours—140 claps a minute, audible at 100 yards," says Ashrita. "Eventually somebody broke my record, but it was just too boring to do again."

Practice Where and When You Can

Ashrita trained for his somersaulting attempts at night on a 200-meter dirt track at his hometown high school. He wore a helmet and a strip of foam to protect his backbone, but still he got covered with mud and grit.

When he decided to try to pogo-stick to the top of the Canadian National (CN) Tower in Toronto, Ontario, he trained on the five flights of stairs in his father's office building.

Spread the News

The folks at Guinness expect you to provide proof of your record. You must have official witnesses; the witnesses can not be friends. One way to get the attention of a local newspaper or radio station is to do your event in a surprising way. When Ashrita attempted the deep-knee-bend record, he did it in a gym (not a surprise), but he rented a baby grand piano and got a friend to play it while Ashrita stood on top, huffing and puffing his way to another record.

GATHER A CROWD

Just because you can't have friends as official witnesses doesn't mean that they can't cheer you on. When Ashrita decided to somersault along the 12½-mile route of Paul Revere's famous "midnight ride" between Charlestown and Lexington, Massachusetts, friends walked alongside him for all 8,341 somersaults to encourage him and keep him from getting run over by traffic.

SET A PERSONAL BEST RECORD, IF NOT A WORLD RECORD

Aim to be the best you can be. Fame does not always bring fortune. Ashrita makes no money for his feats (he works in a health food store); his reward is self-satisfaction.

He insists that there's nothing special about him, and he loves it when someone breaks one of his records. The *Guinness Book* is one route to fame—or a few lines of it. Anyone can get in. Why not you?

Some of Ashrita's Astonishing Accomplishments		
Pogo stick jumping:	Fastest mile: 12 minutes, 16 seconds	July 2001
Stilt walking:	Fastest 8 kilometers (4.97 miles): 39 minutes, 56 seconds	December 2004
Pancake catching:	Most caught in 1 minute: 46	September 2009
Pie throwing:	Most in face in 1 minute: 56	April 2010
Chopstick snapping:	Most in 1 minute: 118	January 2011
Duct-taping oneself to wall:	Fastest time: 2 minutes, 12.63 seconds	October 2011
Banana slicing with a sword on a slackline:	Most in 1 minute: 36	August 2013
Walking on shovels as stilts:	Fastest mile: 24 minutes, 0.25 seconds	March 2014
Skipping rope in clogs:	Most skips in 1 minute: 127	May 2014

TABLE OF MEASURES

LENGTH/DISTANCE

1 inch = 2.54 centimeters
1 centimeter = 0.39 inch
1 foot = 12 inches
1 yard = 3 feet = 0.914 meter
1 meter = 39.37 inches
1 mile = 1,760 yards = 5,280 feet = 1.61 kilometers
1 kilometer = 0.62 mile
1 international nautical mile = 6,076.1155 feet

AREA

1 square inch = 6.45 square centimeters
1 square foot = 144 square inches
1 square yard = 9 square feet = 0.84 square meter
1 acre = 43,560 square feet = 0.40 hectare
1 hectare = 2.47 acres
1 square mile = 640 acres = 2.59 square kilometers
1 square kilometer = 0.386 square mile

HOUSEHOLD

(approx. equivalents)

½ teaspoon = 2 mL
1 teaspoon = 5 mL
3 teaspoons = 1 tablespoon = 15 mL
¼ cup = 60 mL
⅓ cup = 75 mL
½ cup = 125 mL
¾ cup = 175 mL
1 cup = 16 tablespoons = 8 ounces = 250 mL
2 liquid cups = 1 pint = 0.5 liter
2 liquid pints = 1 quart = 1 liter
4 liquid quarts = 1 gallon = 3.78 liters

TEMPERATURE

To convert Celsius and Fahrenheit

°C = (°F – 32) / 1.8
°F = (°C x 1.8) + 32

SPEED/VELOCITY

(mph = miles per hour; kph = kilometers per hour)

1 mph = 1.609 kph
1 knot = 1.150 mph = 1.850 kph

COMPARE CELSIUS AND FAHRENHEIT

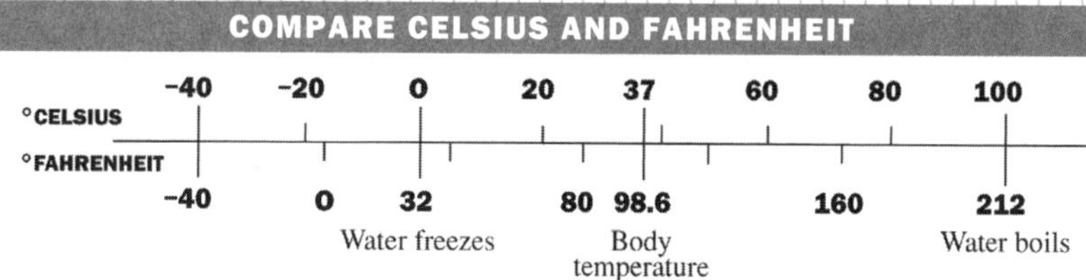

CONVERT INCHES TO CENTIMETERS

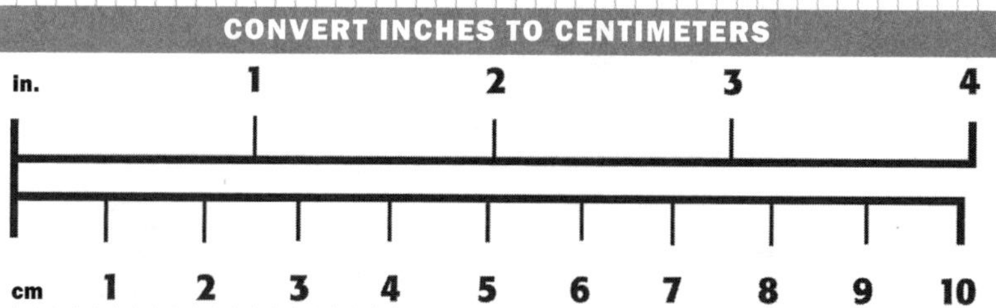

Salt Dough DIY

Like to make things with your hands? Try salt dough modeling. Almost anything can be made with it: decorations, ornaments, jewelry, pots, letters, magnets—the ideas are endless. Most of the ingredients are probably in your kitchen.

You will need:

INGREDIENTS:
- 2 cups all-purpose flour
- 1 cup salt
- 1 cup water
- food coloring (optional)

EQUIPMENT:
- 1 bowl
- 1 spoon
- wax paper (optional)
- airtight container
- rolling pin
- knife
- cookie cutters
- drinking straws
- baking sheet
- toothpicks
- aluminum foil (optional)
- pins

DECORATIONS (OPTIONAL):
- ribbon or cord
- acrylic paints
- paintbrushes
- spray varnish
- magnets
- craft glue

1. Put the flour and salt into the bowl and stir them together. Add one or two drops of food coloring, if using, to the water. Add about ½ cup of water to the flour–salt mixture. Stir to blend. Add more water, 1 spoonful at a time, until the dough is soft. If the dough is dry, add more water, ½ spoonful at a time. If it is sticky, add more flour, 1 spoonful at a time.
2. Spread wax paper, if using, on your work surface. Put the dough on it and knead the dough by folding it over on itself, then pushing the fold away from you. Turn the dough an inch or so after every push, so that you knead a different side of the dough every time. Do this for 10 minutes.
3. Put the dough in an airtight container to rest for 30 minutes.
4. Remove the dough from the container.
5. Preheat the oven to 250°F.

6. Pick a shape and make it.

DECORATIONS

On the work surface, use the rolling pin to spread the dough to ¼ inch thick. (If the dough sticks to the pin, sprinkle it with flour.) Using a knife, cookie cutters, or other shapes, cut out forms. Use a drinking straw to make a hole for a ribbon or cord to go through. Carefully transfer each to the baking sheet.

BEADS

Pinch off portions of dough. Form them into balls. Make a hole for your ribbon or cord by pushing a toothpick through each one. Place on the baking sheet.

A POT

Pinch off a portion of dough (a larger portion for a larger pot). Form a ball. Push your thumbs into the center and, with your fingers around the ball turning it in your hands, press your thumbs into the side. Continue until the pot reaches the desired size. Place on the baking sheet.

continued

- For snakes or to interweave braids, pinch off portions of dough. Using the palm of your hand, roll the dough evenly on the work surface to the desired thickness.
- For letters, pinch off portions of dough and arrange for the letter shapes.

To avoid breakage, make free forms on aluminum foil, then move the foil to the baking sheet.

WHEN YOUR CREATION IS READY . . .

1. Transfer the baking sheet, with your creations, into the oven. Bake until the salt dough is hard and dry. Baking times will vary with the thickness of the dough. Check your dough after about 45 minutes. Pierce any air bubbles with a pin and return the dough to the oven until done. Turn off the heat. Leave dough in the oven to cool.
2. Apply acrylic paint to the crafts. Decorate, as desired. To protect the salt dough from decay, spray with varnish when the acrylic paint is completely dry. Repeat the varnish (if desired) after the first coat of it is completely dry. Glue on magnet(s), if using. String the beads. Wear or display your crafts.

WHAT'S SHAKIN'?

- **To "salt away" means to save.**
- **An "old salt" is an experienced sailor.**
- **The "salt of the earth" is a kind, honest person.**
- **To take something "with a grain of salt" means to not believe it entirely.**

ART-I-FACTS

- **Salt dough sculpture dates from ancient Egyptian times.**
- **Salt deters mice from eating the dough.**
- **In 19th-century Germany, people made inexpensive holiday decorations with salt dough.**

Find 12 Differences

in each pair

Answers on page 190.

ACKNOWLEDGMENTS

PICTURE CREDITS

ABBREVIATIONS:
MB–Media Bakery
NASA–National Aeronautics and Space Administration
PX– Pixabay
SS–Shutterstock
TS–Thinkstock
USLC–United States Library of Congress
WM–Wikimedia

Front cover: (Superhero) Maxim Maksutov/SS. (Cricket) Insima/SS. (Crow) Arto Hakola/SS. (Kids) Luis Louro/SS. (Moose) Drakuliren/SS.

Calendar: 8: MB. 9: (Top) Ravennka/SS. (Bottom) MB. 10: (Top) PlantablesLLC/Etsy. (Bottom left) WM. (Bottom right) PX. 11: (Top and center) TS. (Bottom) NASA. 12: (Background) YarKova/SS. (March font) Bariskina/SS. (Girl) MB. 13: (Top) TS. (Bottom) Vectorart/SS. 14: (Top left) MB. (Bottom right) MB. (Background) Rainer Lesniewske/SS. (Small globes) Kundra/SS. 15: (Top right) TS. (Center and bottom) MB. 16: (Top background) Murina Natalia/SS. (Bottom) C. Quinnell. 17: (Top) Negro Leagues Baseball Museum. (Bottom) TS. 18: (Top) Maxim Maksutov/SS. (Bottom background) TS. 19: (Bottom left) Jennifer Freeman/SS. (Top right) TS. 20: (Top left) WM. (Center left) Great Thoughts Treasury. (Bottom right) TS. 21: (Top) NASA. (Bottom center and right) TS. 22: (Background) Pat Hastings/SS. (Bottom right) TS. 23: (Center left) TS. (Center middle) USLC. (Bottom right) TS. 24: (Top background) Sonia Goncalves/SS. (Bottom) USLC. 25: (Bottom right) WM. (Bottom) Joseph Sohm/SS. 26: (Center) Tony Oshlick/SS. (Background) Afanasia/SS. 27: (Top left) Rido/SS. (Top right) moleday.org. 28: NASA. 29: (Background) Olexiy Bayev/SS. 30: (Center) Dreamstime. (Bottom) WM. 31: TS. 32–33: (Background) Natasha Zalevskaya/SS. 32: Kimazo/SS. 33: BSD/SS. 34–37: (Background) Alex LIli/SS. 34: Moneskom/WM. 35: (Top) Augustas Didzgalvis. (Bottom) greekreporter.com. 36: (Top) calendarcustoms.com. (Bottom) Tduk/WM. 37: Steven Gerner/WM.

Astronomy: 38–39: (Background) Standret/SS. 40: (Top right) Asim Patel/WM. (Bottom left) PX. (Bottom right) WM. 41: (Top background) NASA. (Bottom) 3000ad/SS. 42: (Top) Tsaiproject/WM. (Bottom background) Vadim Sadovski/SS. 43: (Center) Soerfm/WM. (Bottom right) Pavel Chagochkin/SS. 44: (Top) Vadim Sadovski/SS. (Bottom) Cylonphoto/SS. 45: (Background) David M. Schrader/SS. 46: Celestron. 47: (Top) NASA. (Center) BBC News. 48: NASA. 49: (Top) Huntington Library/SuperStock. (Bottom) ESA/Hubble/NASA. 50: (Top) TS. (Center left) Juanco. 51: (Center left) TS.

Weather: 52–53: Nejron Photos/SS. 54: (Top) Julie Delphia. (Bottom) National Weather Service. 55: (Top) TS. (Bottom) TS. 56: (Top) NASA. (Bottom) TS. 57: (Top) Robert Eastman/SS. (Bottom) Sarah Fields Photography/SS. 58: (Top) The Oregonian. (Bottom) TS. 59: (Top) Caleb

Holder/SS. (Bottom) Eric Peterson/WM. 60–61: (Illustrations) Tim Robinson. 62–67: (Background) Petovarga/ SS. 62: (Bottom right) Senoldo/SS. 63: (Top) Nikolaich/SS. (Center right) Tschitscherin/SS. (Bottom) Barandash Karandashick/SS. 64: (Bottom) Vjom/ SS. 65: (Center) Sonia Goncalves/SS. (Bottom) Cozy Nook/SS. 66: (Top) Ati Design/SS. 67: IQoncept/SS.

In the Garden: 68–69: (All) TS. 70: (Top and center) TS. (Bottom) specialty produce.com. 71: (Top and bottom) TS. (Center) Feng Yu/SS. 72: Jenn Huls/ SS. 73: Mira Amaudova/SS. 74: (Top left) PX. (Top right) Olga Savina/SS. (Center) Hofhauser/SS. 75: (Center) Sokolenok/SS. 76: Sokolenok/SS. 77: Jenn Huls/SS. 78: Andrei Verner/SS. 80–81: PX. 82: (Top) PX. (Bottom) Peter M.Dziuk. 83: PX. 84: Hajakely/SS. 85: Jrosenberry1/WM.

Nature: 86–87: (All) PX. 88: Tom Reichner/SS. 89: Dennis W Donohue/ SS. 90: PX. 91: Tom Reichner/SS. 92: Bonnie Taylor Barry/SS. 93: PictureGuy/ SS. 94–95: Eastcott Momatiuk/MB. 96: (All) PX. 97: (Top) PX. (Bottom) Doug Lindstrand/MB. 98: Doug Vinez/SS. 99: Imphoto/SS. 100: (Top left) WM. (Center left) cmarks175. (Center right) P199/WM. 101: TheGreenMan/SS. 102: (Top) PX. (Bottom left) Vitaly Titov/ SS. (Bottom right) Eric Isselee/SS. 103: (Top) Lisa Mann. (Bottom) TS. 104: (All) PX. 105: (Top) Elliotte Rushy Harold/ SS. (Bottom) Preobrajenskiy/SS. 106: (Top) PX. (Bottom) Edwin Butter/SS. 107: (Top) Arto Hakola/SS. (Bottom) Rob Kemp/SS. 108–111: (Background) Lina Truman/SS. (Illustrations) Tim Robinson. 112: Jody Ann/SS. 113: (Top) Valentyna Chukhlyebova/SS. (Center) PX. (Bottom) Lussiya/SS. 114: (Center left) Procy/SS. 115: (Center right) PX.

Health: 116–121: (Background) Laurent Renault/SS. 116: Oksana2010/SS. 117: pbombaert/ SS. 118: (Top) MicroOne/SS. (Center) Barcroft Media. 119: RedlineVector/ SS. 120: Niceregionpics/SS. 121: ekotamak/SS. 122–125: (Illustrations) Tim Robinson.

History: 126: (Sun clock) David Monniaux/WM. (Water clock) Ian Corey. (Hourglass) TS. 127: (Early candle clock) thewellmadeclock.com. (Tower escapement) Rwendland/WM. (Nuremberg egg) Pirkheimer/WM. 128: (Jost Burgi clock) Chris Bainbridge/WM. (All others) TS. 129: (Mechanical alarm clock) Skinner Inc. (Wristwatch) breguet.com. (Chronograph) louismoinet.com. (Stopwatch) tagheuer.com. 130: (Early quartz clock) Museumsfoto/WM. 131: Lorelyn Medina/SS. 132: WM. 133: WM. 134: Eva Bidiuk/SS. 135: Everett Art/SS. 136–141: (Illustrations) Tim Robinson.

Food: 142: Heather Marcus. 143: zefirchik06/SS. 144: Liliya Kandrashevich/SS. 145: (Top) Brent Hofacker/SS. (Bottom) Jenifoto/SS. 146: Karniewska/SS. 147: Osadchaya Olga/SS. 148: Heather Marcus. 149: (Top) Heather Marcus. (Bottom) Sheila Fitzgerald/SS.

Pets: 150–151: Christian Hütter/MB. 152–155: (Background) evgdemidova/ SS. 152: (Top) clipart.com. (Bottom) Aribus/SS. 153: Monkey Business Images/SS. 154: mArt88/SS. 155: (Top) Insima/SS. (Bottom)

Mitch Gunn/SS. 156: Saving Luke/ Facebook. 157: YouTube. 158: PB Media. 159: Denis Grey/AP Photo.

Sports: 160–161: Juergen Hasenkopf/ SS. 162: (Bottom left) Manfred Schotten Antiques. (Bottom right) WM. 163: (Top left) MB. (Top right) West Coast Surfer/MB. 164: Bettmann/Getty Images. (Bottom) Erik Isakson/MB. 165: Ian Walton/Getty Images. 166–171: (Illustrations) Tim Robinson. 172–173: SuperStock. 174: Grendelkhan/WM. 175: Cedar Livestock Festival.

Amusement: 176: (All) TS. 177: AP Photos. 178: (Top) Glenda/SS. (Center) Robynrg/SS. (Bottom) Nanette Grebe/ SS. 179: (Center) Armadillo Stock/ SS. (Bottom) Pavel L Photo and Video/ SS. 180: Luis Louro/SS. 182–184: (All) 13Smile/SS. 185: (Top) 13Smile/SS. (Center) homemadecity.com. (Bottom) firstpalette.com. 186: (Top) Soyka/SS. (Center) Janny2/SS. (Bottom) 13Smile/ SS. 187: (Illustrations) ya_mayka/SS.

CONTRIBUTORS

Jack Burnett: A Big Weight on Their Shoulders, 172. **Alice Cary:** The Curious Crow: Friend or Foe?, 102; A Few Bars About Soap, 116. **Tim Clark:** Myths About the Moon, 50; A Dozen Meteorological Mysteries, 52. **Betty Earl:** Welcome Fairies!, 72. **Mare-Anne Jarvela:** Get Out Your Clams, Peewees, and Taws!, 166. **Kathleen Kilgore:** The Case for a Pet Cricket, 150. **Barbara Mills Lassonde:** Tales of Time Keepers, 126; Animal Heroes, 156. **George Lohmiller:** Tiny Heroes Among Us, 108. **Martie Majoros:** Calling All Birds, 86; For the Love of Tennis, 160. **Harry Edward Neal:** A True "Captain Kid," 136. **Sandy Newton:** Welcome to Our Moose-eum!, 94; Leave It to the Beaver, 112. **Sarah Perreault:** Big Helps for Little Hurts, 122; Bring on Breakfast!, 142; Mouthfuls of Fun!, 146. **Louise Sandback:** Open Your Eyes and Catch a Falling Star, 38; Superstar Teens Make History, 46; Welcome to Our Moose-eum!, 94. **Stephanie Shaw:** Autumn Beaver, 115. **Janice Stillman:** Make Every Day Special, 8. **Heidi Stonehill:** Signs of Change, 62; Swine's Snout and Other Wonders of the Plant World, 80.

Content not cited here is adapted from *The Old Farmer's Almanac* archives or appears in the public domain. Every effort has been made to attribute all material correctly. If any errors have been unwittingly committed, they will be corrected in a future edition.

ANSWERS FROM PAGE 187:

INDEX

ACTIVITIES